PARTY*SLATE*
WEDDINGS
A KEEPSAKE PLANNER

contents

DEFINE YOUR VISION

Getting Started page 8

Planning Ahead page 38

Finding a Venue page 50

MAKE IT A REALITY

Building Your Team page 62

Choosing Décor & Design page 80

Selecting Food & Drink page 110

MAKE LASTING MEMORIES

Creating Celebratory Moments page 128

Engaging Guests page 144

Arranging Weekend Events page 156

Tackling To Dos After the Party page 166

foreword page 4

introduction page 7

photo credits page 170

LEFT Every element of décor plays a role in creating the final vision—from the rented chairs and tables to the florals, lighting, and draping.

foreword

I still remember the first time I met Julie and she shared her vision for PartySlate. It was at an Engage! Summit at The Breakers Palm Beach. All she had at that point was "a PowerPoint and a dream," as she likes to say. From our first conversation, I was inspired by her energy and passion for what she was building. Julie was onto something big—and I was excited that she asked me to be a company adviser.

Julie and her team were on a mission to inspire people planning all types of events and connect them with the best venues, planners, and vendors from around the world. I was wowed by the beautiful PartySlate website, and I loved that I could share my full portfolio of events and credit my talented creative partners.

This book compiles PartySlate's unique perspective on event planning from its trustworthy vendors. Plus, couples will discover insider guidance, advice, and stunning images for every step of the wedding-planning process—a result of the invaluable relationships that the PartySlate team has built as a leader in this space.

As a seasoned wedding and event planner, I love how this book helps everyone—from happy couples to expert vendors—plan a dream wedding. But it's just a glimpse into what PartySlate.com offers couples planning weddings and all of their milestones to come.

This curated keepsake book is one that only Julie and her team could publish, and I'm thrilled that couples beginning their wedding-planning journeys can benefit from the beauty and expertise of PartySlate, both online and in the pages of this incredible book.

Mindy Weiss
Owner, Mindy Weiss Party Consultants

LEFT Ask your photographer about drone options so you can enjoy a bird's-eye view of your perfectly planned affair. The undulating floral hues of this ceremony are beautiful as seen from above.

introduction

I will never forget planning my first big celebration: It was a roller skating and pizza party for my 13th birthday. I can remember it like it was yesterday: that feeling you get when you host a party that means something to you. A spark was lit that day. Over time, I started to think about how I could help people around the world celebrate the moments that matter.

When I started planning large events—from corporate parties to galas and even my own wedding—I would get frustrated by the lack of resources and advice. I would find a beautiful, inspiring photo online, but it would have no information on the vendor team that produced the event. When I clicked on many of those photos, I would find dead ends and broken links. The photos would often be blurry or poor quality. I knew there had to be a better way to help people planning events, especially weddings. That's why I started PartySlate with my cofounder, John Haro.

PartySlate aims to inspire people planning events and connect them with the best venues, planners, and vendors. This book is an extension of that mission, and I couldn't be more excited to share the expertise from our editors in these pages.

In this book, you'll find the guidance I craved when planning my wedding and other large events. Our editors help you define your creative vision (including the first step: selecting your color palette), ask questions when selecting your venue and vendors, understand insider terms, and discover a wealth of ideas for making your wedding uniquely you, all brought to life with stunning photos.

Your journey with PartySlate doesn't have to begin and end here. For all of life's milestones, PartySlate.com will help you find new ideas and the perfect vendor team to bring your vision to life. The website features millions of real wedding and event photos. Each photo includes a full list of vendor credits, including the photographer, planner, and venue, so you can easily find (and hire) the teams that produced your favorite celebrations.

Writing this book has been a true labor of love for the entire PartySlate team and me. To Lauren, Pamela, and Amanda, from the bottom of my heart, thank you for all of your help. I'd also like to express endless gratitude to the vendors who shared advice, insights, and photos of their beautiful work.

And once you have said your "I dos" and the last glasses of champagne have been clinked, we hope you look back on this book as a beautiful memory but also as inspiration for milestones to come.

Julie Roth Novack
CEO and Co-Founder, PartySlate

LEFT A single hue can make a big statement. We love how the peaches and corals in this wedding pop against the arid landscape.

DEFINE YOUR VISION

chapter 1

Getting Started

RIGHT A winding wedding aisle with lush
floral décor feels straight out a secret garden.

envisioning your event

Defining your wedding vision is a highly personal and creative process. If your wedding is a work of art, at this moment it's a blank canvas. Over the course of your planning process, you'll fill it with your creativity and personal touches that are meaningful to you and your partner.

You'll start by painting with broad brushstrokes. What will the look and feel of your big day be? To answer that question, you'll want to explore a few elements, such as color palettes, season, and style.

Color Palettes

Can you picture it? The cool-blue suit of a waiting attendant stands out in the warmth of an orange sunset. Hands gently wrapped around a bouquet of wild lavender. The joyous clink of champagne flutes around a snow-white centerpiece.

Whether they're romantic pastels, lively vibrant hues, or elegant neutrals, the colors you choose for your wedding palette will set the tone, mood, and style of your celebration and help guide and unify your decisions about everything from attire and florals to linen and lighting.

Sonal J. Shah of Sonal J. Shah Event Consultants says, "When crafting a color palette for your wedding that truly speaks to your love as a couple, take inspiration from the places you have traveled together. Consider the rich hues of that enchanting sunset you shared on a tropical beach or the vibrant colors of the bustling market you explored hand in hand. Reflecting on these experiences can help you infuse your colors with a personal touch that evokes wonderful memories."

COLOR COMBINATIONS

Colors are powerful. They evoke feelings and emotions. For example, blues can inspire tranquility and peace, while a vivid orange can energize. When thinking about your wedding colors, focus on how they make you and your partner feel.

Wedding design experts recommend opting for one or two central hues. You can add others as accents, drawing attention where you want it by offering pops of interest. (Of course, rules were made to be broken—so if you're envisioning every color of the rainbow at your celebration, go for it!)

LEFT The metallic elements at this boho wedding ceremony—from the glittery disco balls to the gold flower stands—add instant glamour.

Let Color Theory Inspire You

Color theory is a set of principles that designers and artists use to guide them. It is based on the study of how colors harmonize or mix with one another as well as the warmth or coolness of varied hues and combinations.

Triadic color scheme
Three colors that are evenly spaced on the color wheel at three points of a triangle

ABOVE The couple's attire and stunning *mandap* (covered structure with pillars) nod to their wedding's triadic color scheme.

Want a full-spectrum celebration? Lean on your design team (see p. 71) to help you find a cohesive palette.

Analogous color scheme
Three closely related colors on the color wheel

ABOVE Shades of blue and a touch of light blue-green—all colors from a single side of the color wheel—create a tranquil aesthetic.

Monochromatic color scheme

A single hue with various shades, tints, and tones

....

RIGHT Yellow can be used in any season. This wedding includes vibrant lemon yellows perfect for spring and golden yellows that feel like fall.

Complementary color scheme

Colors on opposite ends of the color wheel that work with (and not against) each other

....

LEFT Choosing pink and green for a destination wedding creates a fresh vibe that evokes Palm Springs, Miami, and the tropics all at once—showing that color can transport or tie in to a locale.

PERENNIALLY POPULAR PALETTES
These central wedding color schemes never go out of style.

- Black and white
- Emerald green and gold
- Navy blue and burgundy
- White and gold
- Sage green and blush
- Dusty blue and white

FIND YOUR PERFECT PALETTE

Inspiration is everywhere! Here are a few suggestions to start brainstorming your color palette.

- **LOOK AROUND** The color choices in your home likely reflect some of your most-loved colors.
- **TAKE INSPIRATION FROM YOUR RELATIONSHIP** Is there a spot that's important to you and your love story? What colors represent that place? You might be inspired by meaningful vacations or trips you've taken together. Consider the aquas, deep blues, and crisp whites of Greece, the rust reds and sandy neutrals of Zion National Park, or the wispy yellows, oranges, and pinks of an epic beach sunrise.

LEFT White and natural rattan chairs pair with delicate blooms at this Tuscan ceremony to create a romantic aesthetic that carries through to every detail.

- **THINK SEASONALLY** Seasons come with their own sets of color associations. Spring colors tend to be light and ethereal. Winter colors, on the other hand, are often dark and bold. Likewise, summer weddings tend to feature more bright lemon, lime, and tangerine citrus tones than the deeper golds and burnt oranges of autumn celebrations.

Shah advises, "Think about the season in which your wedding will take place. Blossoming pastels for a romantic spring wedding or warm jewel tones for a cozy winter affair can bring an extra layer of meaning to your color choices. Combine these seasonal factors with the location of your wedding to create a cohesive aesthetic that pays homage to the beauty of your surroundings. Whether it's the soft blush tones of a garden ceremony or the earthy hues of a rustic barn celebration, let the setting inspire your color palette and make your wedding a true reflection of your love story."

NOTES FOR MY WEDDING TEAM

What Color Schemes Are You Drawn To?

These are some of our favorite color schemes beautifully brought to life, from romantic palettes to bold jewel tones.

Vibrant Palette

This rooftop wedding employs lively hues in a memorable way. The use of color blocking keeps the bright palette from feeling overwhelming by arranging like hues together in beautiful groupings.

Romantic Palette

This romantic wedding wows with warm lighting and a cool palette. The muted pastels marry harmoniously on the tabletops and beyond with varied textures, from velvet linen to sheer voile draping.

PartySlate Tip

Be sure to check the availability of flowers in your chosen palette, especially if you have specific blooms in mind. Seasonality will impact your selection.

Jewel-Toned Palette

Jewel tones evoke luxury. This wedding reception design employs not only rich hues but also gemstone shapes in the form of inspired acrylic menus that infuse even more color.

Garden Palette

Including something blue on the day of is a long-held wedding tradition. This rustic garden wedding puts French blue at the heart of its palette. Lush greenery and bleached wood complete the natural vision.

Classic Palette

Black-and-white palettes are timeless. The color extremes create a dramatic tableau. A touch of pale gray and pink as accent colors add softness to this sophisticated affair.

MONOCHROMATIC MAGIC

Going all in on a single color can create a major wow factor. (You can even take it a step further by requesting that guests dress in the hue or a complementary color.)

While a monochromatic wedding might mean all details are in the same hue, you can also choose shades in the same color family, like light pink, red, and maroon.

To balance out a single strong color, try an undertone of neutrals. Sometimes simply adding cream, white, beige, gray, or the aforementioned metallics can prevent a bold design from becoming too overwhelming.

THIS PAGE Greenery and gold details accent lush cream tables, florals, linen, and walls to create a thoroughly elegant affair.

PERENNIALLY POPULAR SINGULAR COLORS

Thinking about going monochrome? These hues are always a beautiful choice:

- White
- Black
- Sage green
- Royal blue
- Rose gold
- Dusty blue
- Pink
- Lavender

THIS PAGE Choosing a single color like the vibrant pink at this wedding creates a bold yet romantic aesthetic.

Styles and Themes

The wedding terms "style" and "theme" are often used interchangeably, yet their meanings are not the same. Your style is the overarching design of your celebration. It refers to types of aesthetics, such as rustic or romantic. A theme is the guiding wedding concept or the couple's shared interest, such as Hollywood or fairy tales. A theme can be anything that holds meaning for you or that you can dream up. Style and theme work together to create a celebration that captures your love.

For example, a glamorous wedding style naturally complements a Roaring Twenties theme. Or if you and your partner love to explore new places, a travel theme can be beautifully expressed in bohemian style with colorful accents and ornamentation from around the world. If you both love contemporary art, perhaps you'd consider a contemporary art museum–themed wedding with a modern style, including minimal patterns and a geometric arch.

Not every wedding has an overarching theme, but most have a wedding style (or several) they are influenced by. "When choosing your wedding style, look to your home and your lives for inspiration," says Mindy Weiss, an event planner based in Los Angeles who has high-profile clients nationwide. "How do you like to entertain? How do you live? What colors, flavors, or fashion details inspire you every day? Then take details and seasonal elements from your location to marry your style with a strong sense of time and place."

WHAT'S YOUR STYLE?

Becoming familiar with styles and themes can help you hone in on your dream wedding and communicate your vision to your wedding team.

Classic timeless sophistication, as found in a candle-filled ballroom and white linen

Romantic dreamy and ethereal affair with flowing drapery and cascading blooms

Glamorous alluring and enchanting with jewel tones and sparkling chandeliers

Modern chic, minimalist vibes, like an industrial space with mirrored and acrylic elements

Boho free-spirited aesthetic with natural elements like driftwood and succulents

Rustic countryside inspired with local spirits, lanterns, and earth tones

Whimsical quirky and fun, like a string-lit garden full of colorful florals

Style is subjective. Just as fashion expresses personality, your wedding style should reflect you and your partner's relationship. You each might be inspired by different things—every relationship is a beautiful mix of personalities and styles. Combining your ideas will make for a creative expression of your love.

Top planner Marcy Blum of Marcy Blum Events says that when considering your style and theme, "Don't rely on trends that may not make sense for you. Look to things other than weddings for your inspiration."

Use the following style combinations as a jumping-off point. Then add your own special twist, of course.

OPPOSITE This mountain wedding added color with an eclectic mix of whimsical wildflowers and an organic backdrop of pure lavender.

PARTYSLATE

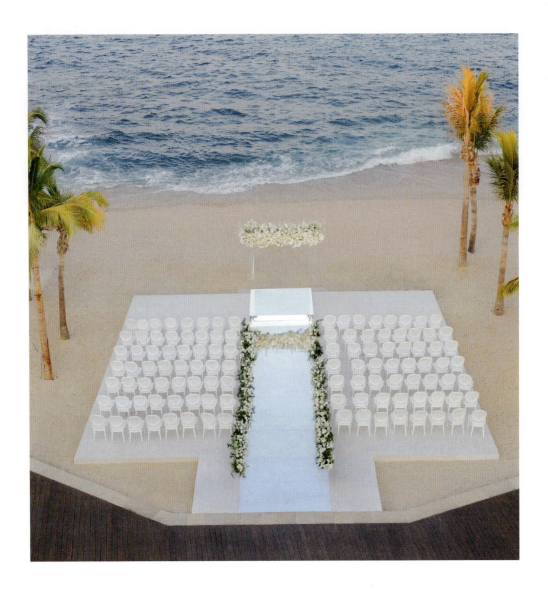

Modern Glamour

HOW IT MIGHT LOOK Your perfect wedding combines a chic, modern space and luxe glamorous details. Imagine a billowing all-white tent, a ballroom with just the right amount of art deco flair, or a flat, wide-open beach. You might opt for a fashionable black-and-white color scheme with gold or silver accents, or choose rich velvets in vivid hues like deep red or navy. Include mirrored details at every turn, from a reflective aisle to glimmering tabletops. Chandeliers dripping in crystals and candles nestled into tall glass votives are a must, as are lush rose arrangements and centerpieces. You'll have a champagne toast, a decadent dinner, and a signature cocktail. Finish with a wedding cake featuring clean lines—and of course, lots of sparkle—then dance the night away to live music.

Rustic Whimsy

HOW IT MIGHT LOOK Your ideal wedding is a marriage of string lights and summer nights. Host your event outdoors or in a vintage barn. You appreciate the simple and natural, so forget about shiny metals, and instead select weathered copper and pewter. Leather and linen chairs outfit lounge areas (with cozy knitted throws to protect guests from chilly nights). Dinner is served at raw-wood tables. The food is locally sourced and prepared with care. Lanterns and candles provide dreamy ambience, and florals include a bit of color and lots of greenery. Live music and craft beer are a given. Send guests home with honey or a tiny evergreen to plant.

PartySlate Tip

Consider metallic accents, white details, and greenery as indispensable neutrals that will round out any color scheme. Gold, silver, and copper bring richness and shine to arches, aisles, and tabletops. Meanwhile white touches and lush greenery will help your other colors stand out.

Romantic Bohemian

HOW IT MIGHT LOOK Your picture-perfect wedding combines eclectic elements with sweet enchantment. The décor is carefree and softly hued, with a chic and muted palette. Sun-bleached pinks and blues pair with pampas grass and wooden tables for a dreamy aesthetic. Satin and linen touches add texture. Don't forget the casual glamour of beautiful blooms and lush greenery cascading off the ends of the tables. The landscape brings in its own décor elements, with garden greens and a colorful sunset. Toast to your love with cocktails served in vintage glassware before digging into wild-caught salmon and mixed grains.

PartySlate Tip

Consider seasonality in the early stages of your planning. For many destinations, the season can make or break your celebration. For example, December in the snowy mountains makes travel difficult, but September offers majestic colors that can complete your vision.

Seasons

There's beauty to weddings in every season—the fresh bounty of spring, the warmth and fun of summer, the dramatic hues of fall, and the cozy romance of winter. There are drawbacks too, including travel complications, additional expenses for in-demand weekends, and unpredictable weather. When you're deciding when to get married, you need to factor in:

- Your personal preferences
- The wedding locale
- Your budget
- The atmosphere you want to create

Finally, are you envisioning an indoor or outdoor wedding? Indoor festivities offer the predictability of being able to celebrate in any season. But if you opt for an outdoor fête, the season becomes a major consideration. So make sure you work with a planning team that has produced outdoor celebrations in your wedding location; they will be familiar with seasonal restrictions and backup plans.

On the following pages, explore seasonal inspiration while considering the opportunities and challenges of each time of year. What feels right to you as a couple? Notice and talk about what draws you in.

ABOVE An autumn wedding in the mountains is the perfect opportunity to capture a cornucopia of vivid color. **RIGHT** Keep your guests cozy with transparent tenting that doesn't sacrifice a single view.

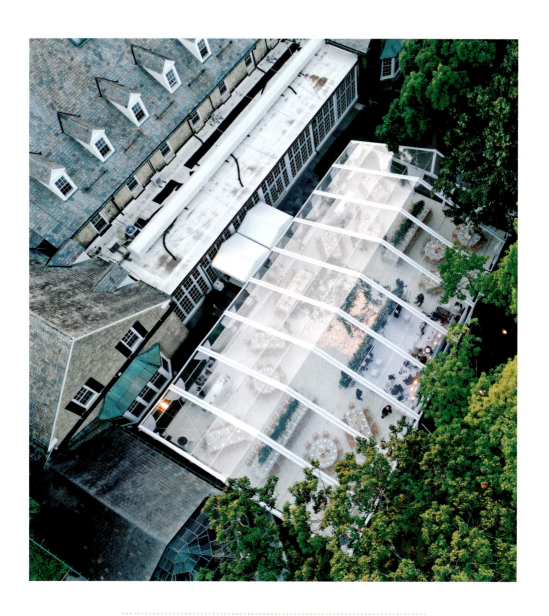

"We wanted a clear plan for the weather, but I also loved the look of a tent. First of all, the structure was beautiful, and the white wood floors that we picked were stunning. We could play with a blank canvas but know that we had a safe option in case it rained. The clear tent allowed the daylight and then the night sky to be visible." —*Caroline, Wisconsin bride*

Fall

THE BEST PARTS
- Crisp air
- Colorful foliage
- Lower risk of inclement weather

THE CHALLENGES
- Fall is a thematically strong season, which might feel limiting in your design
- It's a busy time of year for guests with school starting and holidays approaching
- Fall is the busiest wedding season, so venues and vendors might be more difficult to secure

THIS PAGE Capture the spirit of autumn with thoughtful details like throw blankets for guests, plenty of wood and wicker elements, flannel linen, and fresh fruits. **OPPOSITE** This outdoor reception lets the fall foliage shine with neutral tablescapes and minimal floral décor.

THIS PAGE Bold red hues, moody candlelight, and glamorous gold accents warm a winter landscape with a stark black and white color palette.

Winter

THE BEST PARTS
- Winter landscapes
- Holiday cheer
- Off-peak season (more vendor availability and off-peak rates)

THE CHALLENGES
- The risk of inclement weather can cause travel delays for guests
- It's a busy time of year around the holidays
- Depending on your wedding locale, you may be limited to indoor options

Spring

THE BEST PARTS
- Symbols of new beginnings
- Mild temperatures
- Fresh blooms and greenery

THE CHALLENGES
- Spring brings an abundance of seasonal rain in many locales
- There are unpredictable temperatures during the transition from winter to summer
- Spring break is a popular travel time and causes high travel costs for both domestic destinations and international weddings

THIS PAGE Cultivate a playful spring aesthetic with an assortment of patterned and solid linen—plus fresh blooms galore.

THIS PAGE A summer wedding can embody multiple moods. This wedding starts with a romantic ceremony followed by a tropical reception filled with green palm fronds and a perfectly beachy photo op.

Summer

THE BEST PARTS
- Warm, sunny weather perfect for outdoor events
- Lush greenery and availability of a variety of fresh florals
- More daylight hours for celebrating

THE CHALLENGES
- There is the potential for high temperatures and humidity
- Summer is a busy travel and event season, which means higher rates from venues and vendors
- There's more competition, with venues and vendors in high demand

PLAN B

Outdoor spaces are the most popular wedding venues, so don't completely rule out a nature-set outdoor celebration because of potential weather issues. Here are a few examples for how to plan ahead in case of inclement weather.

Cold or heat Set up portable heaters and offer throw blankets for warmth or electric and hand fans for cooling off.

Excessive sun Construct a canopy or provide your guests with chic paper umbrellas to shade themselves.

Lightning Getting married in thunderstorm season? Remember that tents are not safe from lightning. You must secure an optional indoor space as a backup.

Rain Set up a tent up to three days in advance of your celebration to keep a "just in case" area dry. Add flooring to minimize problems from a rain-soaked ground, and create covered walkways to allow for dry passage between settings.

Wind Make wise décor choices, like avoiding high centerpieces or low-hanging designs. Protect candles with glass votives, and secure table linen. Opt for secured seating chart displays rather than a table of loose place cards.

Questions to Ask Your Wedding Team

☐ What cost considerations should I factor in based on season?

☐ If it's an outdoor event, what backup plans do you have in place in case of weather?

☐ What benefits or drawbacks do you see to weddings in each season?

☐ For our seasonal preference, what destinations would you recommend?

☐ Will seasonal considerations affect guest travel (high travel costs in peak seasons, or potential weather interruptions)?

NOTES FOR MY WEDDING TEAM

chapter 2

Planning Ahead

RIGHT A narrow range of florals, on repeat,
can make a grand statement—like the baby's breath
and lavender blooms at this stunning affair.

Making Your Guest List

Imagine you're standing at the altar with your soon-to-be spouse. You gaze out at your gathered family and loved ones. Whether your wedding day is intimate or large in scale, it is quite possibly the only time in your life that you will have so many of your favorite people in one place. Savor it—and prepare for it.

Building out your guest list is often the most overlooked item in the first stages of wedding planning. Get an idea early on to determine which venues are most suited to your guests' specific needs and your budget.

Marcy Blum recommends that you "craft your guest list carefully, and do your seating intentionally."

Think ahead before you start your guest list. Here's how to approach it:

- **DETERMINE WEDDING SIZE** Before you add any names to your list, think about the size of your dream wedding. Are you hoping for an intimate occasion celebrated with your closest family and friends? Or do you see a grand wedding surrounded by everyone who has made an impact on you and your partner's lives? This vision will help you get a sense of what feels like too many or too few guests.

LEFT Chic rental seating that blends into the sandy scene allows the white aisle and colorful blooms at this wedding to pop.

- **IDENTIFY DEFINITE INVITEES** Begin your list with the people who must be there—for example, your parents, grandparents, and closest friends. As you make your list, think about the can't-miss loved ones you would want present on your special day.
- **KEEP BUDGET IN MIND** Your budget can affect the number of guests you're able to invite, so it's helpful to have at least a range in mind.
- **COMMUNICATE HONESTLY** Be transparent in conversations with your partner about your guest list. Who has been a positive part of your life? Who would you be excited to share moments with on your wedding day? How often will you see or connect with them going forward?
- **ASSIGN A FINAL CUTOFF** It's never fun to make the final cuts but it must be done. Just remember that your wedding day is for you and your partner, and go from there. For individuals and couples who are on the fringe of your list, imagine who will be around to watch your marriage grow in 10, 20, and even 30 years. This step can come later in the process. Finalizing the guest list doesn't have to happen until after you've secured a venue and nailed down your budget. (Your final guest count won't be due until after you've sent invitations and received RSVPs, a few weeks before your big day.) But you'll want a general idea of your number of guests as you search for venues.

PartySlate Tip

If you're creating a guest list in partnership with several parties
(for example, multiple sets of parents), tell everyone how many guests they can add.
This way, everyone feels included and the list is relatively equitable. To avoid
miscommunication, discuss whose list extended family falls under. For example, do
aunts and uncles count toward your list or your parents' lists?

Considering Your Budget

Your wedding budget is going to factor into nearly every decision you make for your celebration, so try to settle on a number early on. First, establish who is hosting or contributing to your wedding. If it's you or your partner's parents, ask them to give you a budget as soon as they can. If it's you and your partner, decide what you're comfortable spending. This information will allow you to make informed choices.

CLOCKWISE FROM TOP LEFT Plan your celebration around a stunning focal point—like an epic ceiling installation. • Small details, such as a flower petal toss, can make for big celebratory moments. • Multi-day celebrations, like this joyful Indian wedding, require a budget for multiple designs and venues.

PartySlate Tip

Getting married at a hotel is very different from getting married at another type of venue. Rentals might be included in the minimum for a hotel, but you may want to swap out their standard chairs for an option that matches your style.

Breaking It Down

Your specific wedding budget allocation will depend greatly on what you value. Are you and your partner foodies who try new restaurants when they open and whom your friends turn to for recommendations? Do you and your partner frequently go see live music or go dancing? Or do you both love to decorate your home and have a vision for your event décor?

If you want to wow with a unique menu or elegant offerings like caviar and lobster, you'll want a budget that can accommodate catering. If, on the other hand, you want to ensure a packed dance floor and offer some surprise entertainment moments, you'll want to budget more in that category. No two weddings look the same, and neither do their budgets.

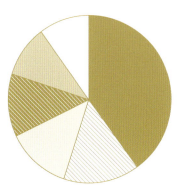

Basic Budget Breakdown for Hotel Weddings

- 40% venue rental and food and beverage
- 15% wedding planner
- 12% photography and videography
- 13% music and entertainment
- 10% décor and flowers
- 10% additional vendors, including invitations, cake, rentals, favors, and tips

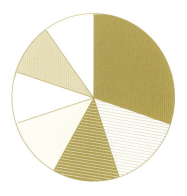

Basic Budget Breakdown for Non-Hotel Weddings

- 30% food and beverage
- 15% wedding planner
- 12% photography and videography
- 13% music and entertainment
- 10% venue rental
- 10% décor and flowers
- 10% additional vendors, including invitations, cake, rentals, favors, and tips

LOCATION IMPACT ON BUDGET

The venue you select will affect how many services and vendors you need to hire. For example, some venues include catering, staffing, and furniture, while others require those teams and items to be brought in. Weddings with ceremonies and receptions at different locations will require transportation for the wedding party and guests, while some venues are all-inclusive and won't need transportation.

Additionally, the location of the venue can greatly influence your wedding cost. For example, a city wedding is often pricier than one in the suburbs or rural areas. Plan for steeper prices in luxury destinations, such as Napa, New York City, and Miami. If you're planning a destination wedding, you may face extra costs for transportation and lodging. Thoroughly research destinations before making any decisions.

Make sure to revisit your budget as you move through the planning process to capture updates and details.

HIDDEN COSTS

Don't let extra costs sneak up on you or your budget. Unaccounted-for expenses often include wedding party gifts, service tax, and vendor tips. They can be as small as postage and as large as hotel room fees and bookings. The best way to ensure that you're not missing any wedding weekend costs is by working with a seasoned wedding planner. They will create a budget spreadsheet for you, help you keep track of your spending, and make expert recommendations as you go. (See page 46 for more on wedding planners.)

ABOVE Ensure your venue offers space for seating and mingling during your reception.

DON'T FORGET

Remember to include these items in your budget planning:

☐ Cultural components
☐ Farewell brunch
☐ Hotel bookings and flights
☐ Marriage license
☐ Personal décor touches
☐ Postage
☐ Rehearsal dinner
☐ Service fees and tax
☐ Valet and vendor meals
☐ Vendor tips
☐ Wedding attire, accessories, and weekend outfits
☐ Wedding party gifts
☐ Wedding rings
☐ Welcome bags and favors

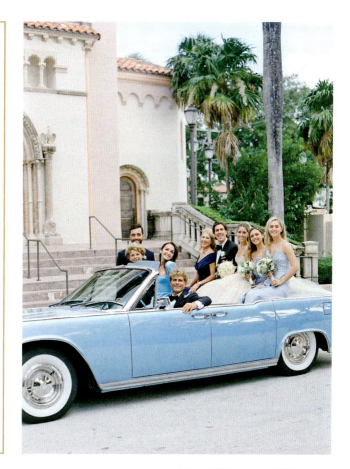

CLOCKWISE FROM TOP Great photo ops—like this family's vintage convertible—don't have to consume a larger portion of your budget. • Show your guests that you appreciate their love and support by budgeting for welcome bags or party favors. • Lean into your venue's natural surroundings, like a sweeping city view, for stunning backdrops.

WHEN TO BOOK
12 to 18 months out

Finding Your Planning Partner

Wedding planners are a must-hire. (Read that again: must hire.) Lock in your planning team as early in the process as possible—and certainly before you book other vendors and choose a venue.

Think of your planner as the executive producer of one of the biggest days of your life. They will know the ins and outs of your wedding day, help you find and keep track of all your vendors, and make sure every moving piece falls into place and is executed to perfection.

An experienced wedding planner will get to know you personally. "I love to get to know my couples. And no two couples are the same in this world," says event planner and wedding expert David Tutera. "I want to know your personalities—who you are, what you love to do. And just as important is knowing what you don't like. Knowing you makes it easier to create beauty for you." Your planner will learn your taste and style and make expert recommendations on every detail of your day. Whether they're brainstorming creative ideas or problem-solving technical issues, having a planner advocate for and with you throughout the process is essential. Not to mention that their behind-the-scenes work on your actual wedding day will give you peace of mind, so you can fully enjoy your experience. Throw in a destination location, and you have a whole other list of tasks to cover.

When you meet with your planner, Tutera says, be honest. "Before you start this journey, share your budget and potential number of guests, and do not provide unrealistic numbers," he says.

ABOVE Your wedding planner will remember details like the parasols to shade guests at these colorful nuptials.

"All of this basic info helps planners to better understand what we may be able to do and what might not be possible."

"The first question to consider is whether or not design is a priority," says Kristin Banta of Kristin Banta Events. She advises thinking about whether you would like a planner and a separate designer or flowers-only team, or a planner who does design in-house. It depends on the complexity of your vision. "If the production is simple, and if a specific vision has already been established, coordination may be sufficient— with the couple and planner leaning more on vendors to independently deliver the vision," she says. "If you're electing to hire a planner/ designer, the body of their previous work and style should resonate with your vision."

The next and equally important consideration should revolve around your connection with the team that you will be working with," Banta continues. "Determine if you will be working with one specific person or several members of a team, and make sure that there is a personal connection and confidence in their professionalism and experience."

Too often, engaged couples forgo a wedding planner in favor of saving room in their budget for other elements. But wedding planners usually save you money in the long run. They will help you get the most out of your budget by creating an in-depth financial guide to follow, recommending vendors that fit into your budget breakdown, and negotiating costs and discounts with industry connections. Planners also make sure you're aware of and prepared for any hidden costs that arise throughout the process—and there will be plenty.

Planners are more than a financial benefit. Hiring a planner will save you time spent on organization, vendor communication, timeline management, logistical planning, and much more. They will anticipate the big

PICK YOUR PERFECT PLANNER

Think about these factors when evaluating the right fit for you.

THEY'RE WELL CONNECTED
Wedding planners should have strong relationships with a network of tried-and-trusted vendors so they can make recommendations for the right team for you.

THEY HAVE GREAT REFERENCES
It's even better if someone you know referred them to you!

YOU LOVE THEIR WORK
Use PartySlate and social media to see what their past events have looked like. Do they inspire you?

YOU CAN BE HONEST WITH THEM
Wedding planners need your genuine feedback. Choose someone you are comfortable enough with to openly discuss everything from your budget to your wedding timeline.

THEY JUST CLICK WITH YOU AND YOUR PARTNER
You'll spend a lot of time with your planner in the months leading up to your wedding. Ensure that you feel like you can ask them anything and call them whenever you need them. Do they make you feel supported from the first meeting?

moments while making sure the details are attended to. Unexpected weather, power outages, late vendors, dress emergencies— you name it—planners have handled it gracefully. Think of your planner as on-site crisis management, and relax knowing your day is in good hands.

Questions to Ask Your Wedding Team

☐ Are you available when we want to get married?

☐ How many weddings do you work on at one time?

☐ What planning services do you provide?

☐ Can you share your references?

☐ What are your areas of expertise or specialty areas?

SPEAK LIKE A PRO

full-service planner a dedicated planner who works with you from inception to completion of your wedding, including venue and vendor selection, budget coordination, and detailed floor plan and timeline creation

host Traditionally, the wedding hosts are the individuals or parties who take on the financial responsibility of the wedding, but increasingly, couples are hosting their own weddings, with full financial and logistical control

month-of planner a planner who takes over the planning roughly a month before your wedding day and who oversees the execution of your wedding on the actual day

NOTES FOR MY WEDDING TEAM

"I found my wedding planner on PartySlate, and she was truly my right hand throughout the entire process. She came up with such brilliant ideas—concepts I would have never thought of myself— that ended up creating some of my favorite moments from my wedding day." —Amanda, *Chicago bride*

chapter 3

Finding a Venue

RIGHT Destination weddings are a
wonderful opportunity to seek out a unique venue
space like this centuries-old chateau.

WHEN TO BOOK
12 to 18 months out

considering spaces

You've thought about colors and themes, and you have an idea of the size of your event and your budget. You have a well-connected wedding planner to help. Now it's time to decide on a location and venue. "Choosing the right venue for your wedding is a personal journey, one that helps define who you are as a couple," says Bryan Rafanelli of Rafanelli Events. "Trust your instincts as you explore the options, and allow yourself to be guided by the connections you feel with each."

As you begin your search, know that the best wedding venues book up quickly, sometimes years in advance, so you might need to have flexibility on your date. Start with settings—places you want to get married—and then consider the venues available. Together with your partner, make a list of what's important to you in a venue. Want a party that lasts all night? Make sure you have a venue without noise ordinances and with excellent sound systems. Prefer a chef-driven dinner? Choose a venue with a chef you love or ensure that the space allows outside caterers.

"Envision yourself walking through the venue, and picture how your guests will feel from the moment they arrive until the final dance of the evening," Rafanelli says. "Imagine the excitement of your grand entrance, the joy of a dance floor that's packed all night long, and the magic of an unforgettable exit under a canopy of sparklers or a mesmerizing drone show."

ABOVE Think beyond the garden and beach and consider lakes and forests for a unique, dreamy ceremony like this one. **OPPOSITE, CLOCKWISE FROM TOP LEFT** Epic views allow for a more minimalist design and subtle décor elements. • A lush lawn leading to an amazing view requires little adornment. • Bring a garden ambiance indoors with dramatic floral installations suspended from the ceiling. Bonus: Enclose the space in dreamy draping. • A venue with high ceilings can accommodate towering centerpieces that allow for conversation across the table.

need to know

Important questions to ask your short list of wedding venues include:

- ☐ What is included in the venue rental fee?
- ☐ Do you have an exclusive or preferred vendor list?
- ☐ Is your venue ADA compliant?
- ☐ Does your venue have décor restrictions?
- ☐ Are there noise ordinances or other sound restrictions?
- ☐ If you provide in-house catering, what is the food and beverage minimum spend?
- ☐ Does the venue have a hard stop time?
- ☐ What audio and visual equipment is available for a DJ or band?
- ☐ Will our wedding be the only event on-site on that date?
- ☐ What extra costs should I account for?

Really think about what each setting could bring to your day. "Consider how the ambiance, lighting, and surrounding scenery contribute to the overall guest experience, ensuring every aspect aligns with your vision," he advises. "Every detail should be thoughtfully considered to ensure a seamless and memorable celebration for you and your guests. Ultimately, the right venue should set the stage for a wedding day that exceeds your wildest dreams."

Settings and Scenery

A setting and its scenery can beautifully enhance your wedding. Outdoor locales like the Colorado mountains or Arizona desert provide stunning backdrops, while urban settings like New York or the Las Vegas Strip give off a palpable energy.

Not sure which setting is right for you? Some couples go with a traditional venue in their nearest big city, while others select a destination halfway around the world. Let your imagination wander (guided by your wedding size and budget).

ABOVE Opt for a wedding aesthetic that matches the spirit of your destination—like this romantic seaside soirée. **RIGHT** Outdoor spots allow for creative layouts and guest flow—so make sure to think outside of traditional seating rows.

SETTING SPECIFICS

In addition to the look, assess the feel of the setting you choose. If you select a venue in the mountains, for example, consider how the altitude might affect you and your guests. Advise guests on the potential impact, and make sure to have bottled water on hand to keep everyone hydrated. A desert wedding may start out warm and sunny during your wedding ceremony, but by the time your reception begins, temperatures will likely have dropped significantly. Prioritize amenities to keep your guests comfortable.

"We love traveling and going on new adventures, and getting married felt like the biggest adventure we'd gone on so far, so it felt right to do it in a new-to-us destination. We were looking for somewhere that had a little bit of everything—from historic cities to warm beaches to rolling vineyards—and Portugal fit the bill perfectly and gave us a built-in honeymoon." —Chelsea, **destination bride**

POPULAR WEDDING VENUES

Consider these types:

- Beach resorts
- Gardens
- Hotel ballrooms
- Hotel event spaces
- Industrial venues
- Museums and cultural landmarks
- Outdoor rooftops
- Raw loft spaces
- Restaurant private dining spaces
- Vineyards and wineries
- Waterfront patios

Types of Wedding Venues

Your setting preferences may steer you to a choice of venue. Couples getting married in a large city might end up at a luxury hotel, a bustling restaurant, or a rooftop. Others who have always imagined a wedding in wine country usually find a vineyard or an outdoor spot.

Perhaps you've always imagined getting married in a certain type of venue. A church, a synagogue, or a mosque might be important to you and your partner. A historical or cultural landmark like a museum could be a compelling venue to you, or maybe you're drawn to a raw industrial event space.

Your desired level of convenience might also drive your decision. Hotels, resorts, and restaurants often include more tables, chairs, and linen in the rental fee, for example, while raw spaces require outside rentals and coordinating with more vendors. Likewise, hotels and resorts offer multiple event space options, while landmarks, rooftops, and raw spaces often have one or maybe two areas to choose from.

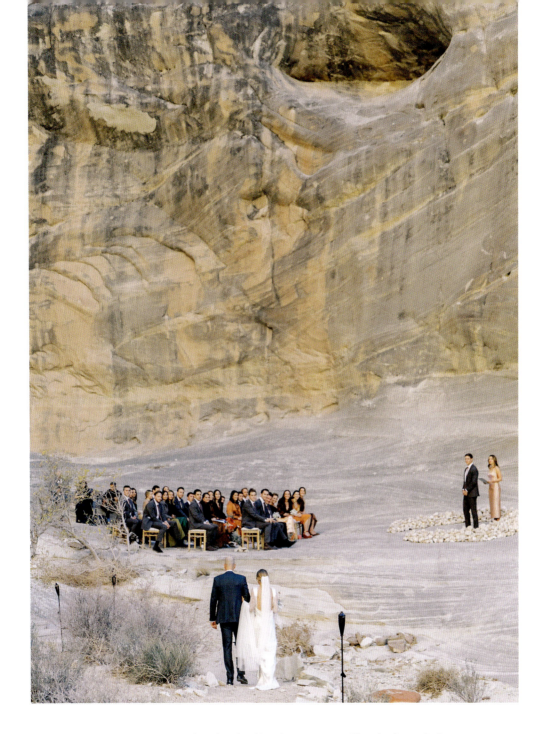

ABOVE Sweeping outdoor locales like this one can still make for an intimate wedding ceremony. **OPPOSITE FROM TOP** Tented venues are a perfect opportunity for awe-inspiring ceiling décor installations. • Sandy-toed nuptials may require permits—so consider a venue with its own waterfront location and private beach.

OUR NECESSARY AMENITIES

What amenities are important to you as a couple?

☐ Chairs, tables, and basic rentals included

☐ Preferred or exclusive caterer

☐ Outside food and beverage allowed

☐ Vegetarian, kosher, or another option

☐ Greenroom or wedding suite

☐ On-site venue coordinator

☐ ADA compliance

☐ Picturesque photo-op spots

FROM TOP Elegant chair rentals can elevate any wedding ceremony. • Rooftop views wow and pretty pink florals and décor stand out too.

Amenities

As you're drawn into the scene and setting of possible venues, make sure to find out what amenities are offered. Consider not only what's important to you as a couple but also what would be helpful for your wedding guests. What will make you and your guests feel comfortable, secure, and taken care of?

Amenities are especially important for people with certain restrictions. For example, if you have guests with food allergies, a venue's caterer needs to be able to offer safe meal options. If you have guests with physical restrictions, talk to your venue about how they will be accommodated throughout the event. If you have older guests with mobility considerations, make sure your venue has easy parking on-site.

FROM TOP Maximize shade with additional umbrella vignettes and canopied seating for guest comfort. • If you want an epic entrance (or exit), a grand staircase should be on your amenity list.

Questions to Ask Your Venue Team

☐ What's the venue's guest capacity?

☐ Does the venue hold more than one wedding a day?

☐ What deposits are needed and when?

☐ What is the refund policy?

☐ What services are included?

☐ Is there a list of preferred vendors, or may we bring in anyone we'd like?

☐ What are the parking and valet options and related costs?

SPEAK LIKE A PRO

ADA compliance a venue is ADA (Americans With Disabilities Act) compliant if they offer access to all individuals with disabilities

exclusive vendors a list of vendors you must select from when hosting your wedding at a particular venue

hard stop the time by which your wedding must end without any extensions or negotiations; time depends on staffing, noise ordinances, and more

in-house a term used to describe items that your venue provides, from tables and linen to catering services and event planning

preferred vendors a list of wedding vendors that your venue prefers to work with, likely because of established relationships or previous experiences

venue coordinator an individual who works for the venue and is available on-site to assist with logistics and coordination

venue walk-through an opportunity to visit your shortlist of wedding venues in person, ask any questions, and envision your wedding in the space

NOTES FOR MY WEDDING TEAM

ABOVE Make sure your rooftop venue has an elevator for guests who need assistance with stairs.

MAKE IT A REALITY

chapter 4

Building Your Team

RIGHT With a little planning, your ceremony exit can be as memorable as your entrance. This couple's petal toss was magic.

beginning your search

Your venue is booked and the date is saved. Your wedding planner is on board. It's time to hire the rest of your vendors. The professionals on your team must fit into your budget, meet your needs, match your taste, and most important, be available on your now-set wedding date.

Victoria Dubin of Victoria Dubin Events shares, "When our clients begin to navigate the wedding-planning process, we encourage them to share as many details and personal facts about themselves as possible, so that we can recommend vendors that we know will help create a wedding experience that is a personal reflection of the couple's taste and style."

Some vendors also book up years out. As you work with your planner to build your team, you'll want to prioritize outreach by availability. Vendors like photographers and bands can typically work only one event a weekend, and therefore book more quickly, while larger-scale décor companies book multiple weddings in a single day and can often be more accommodating.

Though the idea of curating a wedding team from scratch may feel daunting, online planning platforms like PartySlate have the necessary tools to discover companies that service your wedding's locale. On PartySlate, you can search by vendor category, location, pricing, event type, and diversity, then view the wedding portfolios of the companies that fit your criteria. You can also review company connections to determine which vendors have previously worked at your venue or have worked together on previous weddings.

....

RIGHT Ask whether your photographer and videographer offer add-on services such as drone images and footage.

BOOKING AHEAD
Select vendors in this order:

Wedding planner: They will help you select the best venue and have recommendations for vendors they've worked with. (See page 46 for more about wedding planners.)

Venue: These often book out well over a year in advance, and they can lead you to vendors they have previously collaborated with. (See page 50 on booking your venue.)

Photographer/Videographer: If you have a specific photographer or videographer who aligns with your style preferences, book early. (See more on page 66.)

Entertainment: Whether you want a band or a DJ, secure them early to ensure you get the one you want. (See more on page 68.)

Once you choose these vendors, you can move on to selecting a floral and design team, a caterer, a stationery company, and more. These vendors are often able to handle multiple events at a time and therefore have more availability.

SUGGESTED BOOKING TIMELINE
12 to 18 months out
☐ Wedding planner
☐ Venue (and caterer)
☐ Photographer
☐ Entertainment, especially if there's a specific band or DJ that you want

8 to 12 months out
☐ Design/décor/floral company
☐ Hotel blocks
☐ Caterer (if not provided by venue)

6 to 8 months out
☐ Stationery/print company
☐ Bakery

WHEN TO BOOK
12 to 18 months out

Photographer and Videographer

You've likely heard it before: Your celebration will fly by. Hiring the right photographer and videographer is so important. Their work catches and freezes each fleeting moment—so you can relive your favorite memories whenever you want.

You *must* love your photographer's work, and you also need to feel comfortable with your photography team. You will arguably spend as much time on your wedding day with your photographer as you will with your partner, because they will capture every moment from getting ready through goodbyes.

Yes, you should hire a videographer too. A videographer will catch all that magic live so you can share it with family and friends and cherish it for years to come. Whether it's a full-length feature or a sizzle reel, your videographer's work will offer unseen perspectives and guest interactions you didn't get to witness the first time. Plus, you'll be able to listen to your partner's vows and loved ones' speeches all over again (and again). Good photographers are attentive and helpful when needed but also blend into the background and let natural moments unfold.

PartySlate Tip

Look at work akin to your wedding when choosing a photographer—for example, outdoor albums or indoor photos that match your setting. For videographer selection, consider what you want to include, from rehearsal dinner or brunch coverage to drone footage or social media teasers.

need to know

Important questions to ask potential photographers and videographers include:

- ☐ What is your photography (or videography) style?
- ☐ Do you have sample galleries from weddings you have worked at my venue?
- ☐ How do you make your couples feel comfortable while shooting?
- ☐ When can we expect final edited photos and videos after the wedding?
- ☐ Do you offer any packages that include photo albums or other services?
- ☐ What is your favorite moment throughout the wedding day to shoot and why?

LEFT Make sure to look at a photographer's portfolio of work—from first-look photos to action shots—to ensure the team can create and capture moments that are important to you.
BELOW Lighting is an essential element of joyful images, so make sure you choose a photographer who can work with the ever-changing natural light at an outdoor wedding.

WHEN TO BOOK
12 to 18 months out

Entertainment

Entertainment is one of the most-remembered elements of a wedding. From the start of your ceremony to the last moment of your reception, music helps shape your celebration.

When it comes to the reception, the biggest entertainment decision to make will be whether you want a live band or a DJ (with or without an MC)—or both. Your musical vendors will make sure to get your guests on their feet and keep the dance floor full, but they'll also ensure that every special moment happens on schedule and moderate the mood of your gathering. An experienced DJ or band will know what to play to keep the joyful energy high while fostering conversation during cocktail hour; they'll know the perfect dinner music; and they'll know how to fill a dance floor and how to punctuate the evening with moments that will get guests out of their seats.

LEFT A painter provides guest entertainment as well as art you'll keep forever. **RIGHT** Nothing fosters guest engagement like live music and a wow-worthy dance floor.

need to know

Important questions to ask potential entertainment providers include:

- ☐ How far in advance do your available dates book up?
- ☐ Do you have entertainment options for the ceremony, the cocktail hour, and the reception?
- ☐ For bands or DJs, how do you work with your couples to customize a song list?
- ☐ For bands or DJs, how many hours of entertainment do you include in your packages?
- ☐ For bands or DJs, are you available for after-parties?
- ☐ For bands or DJs, does your service include an MC or would we need to book someone separately?

PARTYSLATE

BAND OR DJ, OR BOTH?

Both live bands and DJs bring celebratory energy to your event. Deciding between the two—or whether to go with both—comes down to a few factors.

- **YOUR TASTE IN MUSIC** Each band has a certain sound, style, and repertoire of songs they've rehearsed, and you'll want to find one that fits your taste and needs. DJs, on the other hand, have an almost endless library of music at their fingertips.
- **THE ENERGY OF YOUR EVENT** Live bands are dynamic and bring their own power to the stage, which can have an electrifying effect on a crowd. A DJ spinning tunes may not be able to move around as much but can more quickly change up the beat depending on what the crowd needs or wants.
- **SETUP AND SPACE** Bands need enough space to fit their members and equipment, plus a stage, lighting, and more. DJs take up less space and have more limited equipment.
- **BUDGET** Live bands, because they often have many members, tend to be more expensive than DJs, who usually work solo or with a partner.

Still can't decide? You may not need to! Many couples opt to have a band for part of the reception and then transition to a DJ.

DO I NEED AN MC?

A master of ceremonies, or MC, walks a fine line between entertainment and event coordinator. MCs make the event run smoothly: They make formal announcements and communicate information to prevent guests from getting confused. They also keep the events of your reception on schedule and can read the room and engage the crowd as needed.

WHEN TO BOOK
8 to 12 months out

Caterers

Many believe the way to your guests' hearts is through their stomachs—and it all starts with a seasoned caterer. Some venues, like hotels and restaurant event spaces, have in-house catering. Others have lists of preferred caterers that they require you to choose from. But many wedding venues will give you the freedom to choose your catering company. No matter how you source your food and drink, doing a tasting will help you shape the entire menu. (Find more delicious details about tastings and service in Chapter 6.)

PartySlate Tip

Once you've narrowed your caterer list, you can make your final choice by scheduling a tasting. There may be a small fee, but it's worth it.

need to know

Important questions to ask potential caterers include:

☐ What services and rentals do you provide, in addition to the food?

☐ Have you worked an event at our venue before?

☐ What catering specialties are you known for that set you apart from other caterers?

☐ Which catering styles do you offer (plated, passed, family style, stations, other)?

☐ What is your pricing structure—per person or package?

☐ Can you meet our guest list needs?

☐ How do you accommodate guests with dietary preferences or restrictions? (Ask about specific dietary accommodations you know your guests will need.)

ABOVE Consider event flow when curating your menu. Does your venue have space for a buffet, food stations, or both? **RIGHT** Venues might lend themselves more easily to specific styles. Work with your design team to make sure your venue can easily accommodate your wedding aesthetic.

WHEN TO BOOK
8 to 12 months out

Florists and Designers

Your design and décor team will create and execute the overall aesthetic of your wedding. Their goal is to bring your vision to life and align every detail with your theme, palette, and style. Their work is also the first thing guests will notice as they step into your ceremony and reception space, and it will be the backdrop of countless photos.

As you search for décor partners, think about these questions:

- Do you want to be floral forward? If so, consider working closely with a florist.
- Does your vision include lots of lighting, installations, and nonfloral décor? Then a design company with in-house lighting and draping teams that partners with a florist may be the best fit.
- What lighting and staging does your venue offer? Share this information with your décor team.

need to know

Important questions to ask potential florists and designers include:

☐ Can we see a mood board of your vision?

☐ Do we have the option to come in person to see a sample of floral arrangements, centerpieces, and other décor?

☐ What flowers do you recommend for my wedding season?

☐ In addition to flowers, what other elements do you have to complement the décor, like votives, lanterns, lighting, and more?

Print Design

Save-the-dates and wedding invitations are the first introduction your guests will have to your big day. Ceci Johnson of Ceci New York advises, "To achieve a cohesive wedding, couples should establish a theme or color palette, use consistent typography and imagery across all stationery, and create a personalized monogram."

Before you get started with an invitation designer, think through what you need. The company you use for save-the-dates and invitations will most likely be your go-to creator for the rest of your wedding day signage and print items.

Save-the-dates will be your initial communication with guests. Consider using your engagement photos, a sketch of your wedding venue, or a QR code that leads to your wedding page.

The second piece of mail you send holds more weight (literally and figuratively, so don't forget to budget for stamps). There's no better way to get your family and friends excited for your event than by sending a well-designed invitation. Johnson adds, "Extend your invitation's design to your venue décor, signage, and more to ensure a unified look from save-the-date cards to the event itself—we call this event branding." A full communications suite for your wedding could include:

- Save-the-date cards
- Invitation suite
- Programs
- Bar signage
- Place cards
- Table numbers
- Menus
- Thank-you stationery

WHEN TO BOOK
6 to 8 months out

need to know

Important questions to ask potential invitation and print designers include:

☐ What special details will make our invitation suite feel uniquely ours?

☐ Do you offer postage and mailing of the invitations?

☐ What other printed items do you recommend for a wedding celebration?

☐ Can we use your design in other elements at our wedding, like the dance floor, bar, and linen?

PARTYSLATE

ABOVE Citrus hues and tropical flowers from the print suite tease the décor for the big day, with prints carrying through to the dance floor, stations, and flower arrangements.
LEFT A wedding invitation suite can accommodate more than one motif, so don't be afraid to mix and match (and feature your furry friends).

The Suite Life

A full print suite starts with your invitations and threads throughout your big day by incorporating complementary design elements on each piece of printed material. Here are a few examples from PartySlate couples and why we love them.

A monogram design combining partners' first initials makes invitations very personal. Combined with foliage-and-floral inspiration, the personalization offers guests a glimpse of style and theme.

Handsome, modern, and with a pop of color, these sophisticated invitations come together with creative font use, envelope liners, and belly bands—long paper that wraps around multiple pieces of stationery—secured with wax seals.

PartySlate Tip

Calendars fill quickly. Send your save-the-dates six to 12 months in advance (the further out the better for destination weddings). Meanwhile, invitations can go out around three months in advance, with RSVPs due around one month out, when you will need to finalize your head count with your venue and some vendors.

Cheerful hues in complementary colors feel like a celebration from the moment a guest opens the envelope.

These save-the-dates immediately convey a sense of place and let guests know they're in for a weekend of fun.

This marsh wedding invitation created a moody vibe with art that carried over from its envelope liner to its response card.

Gorgeous watercolors reflect the stunning locale of this wedding and showcase wedding colors in vivid blues, greens, and yellows.

Supporting Vendors

Once you've lined up your big players—your planner, photographer, videographer, entertainment, florist, caterer, and invitation designer—it's time to fill in the details. Your planner will guide you through booking these vendors and services.

- **BAKERY AND CAKE MAKERS** In addition to your cake, your bakery can provide your full dessert spread if you choose. *Book six months in advance.*
- **HAIR, MAKEUP, AND STYLISTS** This team will keep you and your wedding party looking your best for the hundreds of photos you'll be in. *Book nine months in advance.*
- **AUDIO/VISUAL AND TECHNOLOGY COMPANIES** Your band or DJ is only as good as everyone's ability to hear and see them; you may need to augment your

LEFT Work with your rentals team to choose elements that elevate your wedding style, like these chic seats. **OPPOSITE FROM TOP** A stand-alone seating chart can double as stunning photo op and party favor station all-in-one. • Ask your baker for their creative ideas. This bakery exceeded expectations with perfect personal cakes.

venue's capability for the best experience. *Book 12 months in advance.*
- **RENTALS (TABLETOP ITEMS, LINEN, FURNITURE, BARWARE, AND MORE)** Your design team will help you choose rentals that will complement your aesthetic, from lounge décor and seating to tabletops and even glasses for toasting. *Book 10 months in advance.*
- **STAFFING COMPANIES** From coat check staff to the servers who will interact with your friends and family at their tables, a good staffing company makes a big impression. *Book six months in advance.*
- **VALET, PARKING, AND TRANSPORTATION** Give some thought to how you will get your guests from here to there in comfort. Your venue may offer valet or parking options, or staffing teams can help. *Book six to eight months in advance.*

Questions to Ask Yourself

What décor elements are important factors in your dream wedding vision? Some common ones are:

☐ Backdrops
☐ Candles/ambient lighting
☐ Chandeliers
☐ Dance floor
☐ Draping
☐ Florals
☐ Installations

PARTY*SLATE*

Questions to Ask Your Wedding Team

☐ **FOR ALL VENDORS** Have you worked at our venue or with any of our other vendors before?

☐ **FOR ALL PHOTO, VIDEO, AND DESIGN VENDORS** Can we see galleries of your recent wedding work?

☐ **FOR ALL PHOTO, VIDEO, AND DESIGN VENDORS** Can we see examples of your work in weddings of a similar size and style as ours?

☐ **FOR PHOTO AND VIDEO VENDORS** Will you have assistants working with you on our wedding day?

SPEAK LIKE A PRO

invitation suite a package of paper goods that are mailed with your wedding invitation, often including response card, accommodation details, rehearsal dinner or welcome party invitations, and directions or location information

load-in and setup when vendors—such as rental companies, florists, and entertainment companies—will deliver and set up their equipment on the day of your wedding

lounge vignette an arrangement of furniture, tables, and décor that provides a gathering space for guests at your cocktail hour or reception

tasting a sampling of potential appetizers, entrées, dishes, and cocktails or mocktails that your caterer or venue curates to help you select your final wedding menu

vendor meal a meal that you provide for your vendors to ensure that they are fed during their long day of work

---

NOTES FOR MY WEDDING TEAM

ABOVE Ask your wedding team for recommendations on how to best utilize your space for perfect seating—be it rows, vignettes, stacked, geometric, or serpentine table arrangements.

chapter 5

Choosing Décor & Design

RIGHT Bring your wedding design to life
with a vivid entryway that whisks your guests
from the mundane to the celebratory.

the ceremony

Picture the moment you say "I do." The ceremony will reflect your love, your relationship, your values, and your hopes for the future. It also kicks off your celebration.

Aisles
Create a Beautiful Walk to Remember

This is it: All the dreaming, planning, and decision-making has led you to this moment, your first steps toward making it official with your loved one.

Whether you are walking up the aisle to join your partner or are watching your soon-to-be spouse walk toward you, the ceremony aisle is the setting for some of the day's most meaningful moments. Your aisle design ultimately depends on several factors—your overall wedding style, of course, but also your venue size and ceremony tone. Plus, you'll want to make an entrance!

LENGTH AND SHAPE

Your venue is your first consideration for aisle design. What lengths or shapes of aisles can the space accommodate? You'll have different options if you're getting married in a sprawling garden than if you're saying "I do" in an intimate ballroom.

Here are some other considerations you will need to discuss.

- **GUEST COUNT** You'll want an aisle that's long enough to seat all of your guests comfortably while keeping them close enough to witness your vows.
- **CEREMONY AMBIENCE** A longer aisle means a longer procession and an opportunity for a little more drama. A shorter aisle can feel more intimate and cozy.

- **AISLE SHAPE** Traditional aisles tend to be straight walkways from entrance to arch. Less traditional options include serpentine aisles that meander and ceremonies in the round, which allow for closer views from all angles.

AISLE DESIGN

An aisle is more than just the space between chairs, and you can opt for more than a simple runner. Think of this area as a blank canvas that you can dress up or down depending on the feel you want to create. The material of the aisle floor, décor flourishes, and guest seating will all work together to create your ceremony's ambiance.

Let your wedding style inform you. For example, for a boho vibe, consider overlapping rugs in vibrant hues and textured weaves. Want a touch of glamour? A mirrored aisle is a stunning option that reflects lighting and décor. A walkway of petals is pure romance. You can also lean into elements of your venue. For example, if

....

OPPOSITE FROM TOP LEFT Ombré or color blocking adds a whimsical touch to a curated wedding aisle. • Multiple wedding arches result in a beautiful—and memorable—walk up the aisle. • Opt for colorful favors for a photo-worthy wedding ceremony that puts guest comfort first. • A neutral aisle and seating allows vibrant florals to lead guests' eyes to the beautiful arch.

PARTY*SLATE*

82

USE YOUR SURROUNDINGS

Incorporate existing venue infrastructure and décor for your aisle, such as:

Staircases
Gracefully descend to say your vows.

Gardens
Let existing greenery define your outdoor aisle.

Carpets
Patterns or prints can center your aisle.

Pathways
Stone or paved paths can offer a rustic aisle.

LEFT Mix and match styles—like whimsical cotton candy-hued blooms with sleek modern seating—for optimal effect. **RIGHT** An abbreviated ceremony and chic, cozy blankets for guests make a winter wonderland wedding memorable (not to mention that view, doubled in the mirrored aisle).

your ceremony is in a garden, keep it natural with a grass aisle flanked by planted florals on both sides. For a beach wedding, rake the sand into a pretty design, like whimsical swirls or a modern herringbone pattern. For unique indoor settings, let the rustic hardwood floors or Moroccan tiles of the space you've chosen create your path.

You'll also need to think about how to frame your aisle. Florals at the end of each row of seats is a common choice. You can also consider lining your aisle with candles, lanterns, or greenery—or keep it minimal and sleek with no added décor.

CEREMONY SEATING

This is where form meets function. Guests will need a comfortable place to observe the ceremony, and the chair design should blend with the ambiance you're creating with your aisle and other décor. Many venues provide seating options. But if their choices are limited or don't align with your style, chair rentals are a great alternative.

Keep the potential needs of guests with mobility considerations top of mind when planning your seating. That might mean anything from reserving a space for a wheelchair to widening your aisle.

THOUGHTFUL TOUCHES

Think about your guests' comfort by placing items on their seats, such as:

Paper umbrellas for a sunny day	Rattan or folding fans for warm climates	Shawls or light throws for chilly weather

Arches

Frame Your Nuptials

Imagine saying your vows in a lush forest between two towering trees casting speckled light through their canopies, or in an elegant ballroom with a flawless floral backdrop. Your arch is where you will join your life with your partner's. It will be the backdrop against which you'll stand in front of your loved ones and smile, maybe shed a few tears, and have (at least) one epic kiss.

On top of all that, your wedding arch is an important decorative element that will be captured in just about every image during your ceremony. Eddie Zaratsian, artist, designer, educator, and creator of Eddie Zaratsian Lifestyle and Design, says, "I remind my couples that the ceremony should maintain a timeless feeling to it and that they should work with their surroundings. Elements and décor should frame the couple rather than overpower them."

ARCH DESIGN

The term *arch* is a bit misleading. Sure, your ceremonial structure might be an arc shape, but it could also be a full circle, a square—or no shape at all. A rectangular arch is classic and traditional; the shape represents stability, and its four corners are linked to the four corners of the earth.

PartySlate Tip

We recommend being surprised by your design rather than seeing it ahead of the ceremony. Your aisle design will surely wow your guests, but we love when couples are the ones to lose their breath at the first sight of their own ceremony design.

Circular arches represent the circle of life and continuity. Couples are also creating interest with unusual forms that still nod to the idea of an arch. For example, triangular arches—representing a union of body, mind, and spirit—have become popular, as have asymmetrical arches which suggest being free-spirited and future exploration.

In fact, more and more, couples are getting creative and using "no arch" arches. Imagine free-form cascades of florals as a backdrop or an open circle of pampas grass seemingly sprouting from the ground with nothing overhead or behind you as a vow setting. Or consider florals twining around two rustic wooden columns that are unjoined at the top, creating a beautiful focal point.

You may choose to have your arch style match your wedding locale—like a rustic wooden arch adorned with sunflowers in a field next to your barn reception space, surrounded by your guests seated on benches. Or you might decide to play with contrasting styles and, in that same field setting, instead opt for a modern, mirrored square arch that reflects nature while guests sit in transparent ghost chairs.

Close your eyes and picture your moment. What do you see?

OPPOSITE, CLOCKWISE FROM TOP LEFT

An arch with depth adds drama from every angle. • An arch with practiced asymmetry can be especially eye-catching.• A unique palette can wow with a riot of bright organic hues. • Combine styles with a structured rectangle arch—then double the beauty by layering two arches.

PartySlate Tip

If your venue has a scenic view, position your aisle and arch to take advantage of that natural focal point.

Additionally, you might want to follow religious or cultural traditions when choosing your arch design. For example, a *mandap* is a ceremonial structure built for Hindu or Jain weddings. Mandaps were traditionally made from wood, but newer designs often incorporate draping, flowers, and crystals. This ceremonial altar consists of four pillars symbolizing the four elements: earth, water, fire, and air. There should be room under the canopy for you and your soon-to-be spouse, your officiant, and your immediate family, as well as for certain rituals to unfold.

Jewish couples exchange vows under a chuppah. A chuppah also has four posts, representing the couple's home together. The arch's open sides evoke hospitality and the welcoming of loved ones and blessings. Often, a chuppah will feature a family heirloom in the form of a prayer shawl (tallit) in its design. Modern Jewish couples might opt to match their wedding palette rather than a traditional white chuppah.

ABOVE This couple said "I do" under an arch that extended the greenery of their natural setting.

make it yours

Make your ceremony unique by adding personal elements like monograms, remembrances, custom embroidery, or artwork that holds meaning for you. Make a statement for everyone to see, or keep it small and in an area that only you and your partner are privy to.

CLOCKWISE FROM TOP

An elegant monogram can personalize your aisle. • Weave family in by embroidering edges of a veil with family members' wedding dates. • Pin a photo of a loved one to your bouquet. • Create a discreet memorial to carry a lost loved one with you. • A monogrammed fan adds a personal touch to guest comfort.

PartySlate Tip

Ask potential designers if they have experience with your specific traditions and to see examples of their relevant arches.

One Space, Five Styles

Take a look at how the same space can be transformed depending on your wedding style and design team's talents. Here's the iconic Colony Hotel in Palm Beach five different ways.

ROMANTIC
The curves of the natural-wood seats and the white wisteria blooms swaying in the breeze from the pink floral-laden arch are pure romance.

MODERN
Modern wedding styles feature clean, minimal elements, like this wedding's acrylic columns that frame the aisle's entrance and arch.

CLASSIC
A classic wedding features design elements that embody tradition and never go out of style, like this crisp floral arch and white chairs with overhead string lights.

UNIQUE
A unique wedding overturns tradition, like this ceremony design, which went all in on tropical greenery and an ombré of pink hues, from soft to vivid.

GLAM
Nothing says glamour like a mirrored aisle. Flank it with lush pink florals and smoky gold seating, and you've got a stunning scene like this one.

Bouquets and Boutonnieres

Showcase Your Style Through Your Accessories

Wedding parties have been carrying and wearing flowers for centuries. The tradition dates to ancient times and has several origin stories; flowers have long symbolized new beginnings and hopes for the future. Today bouquets and boutonnieres are the ultimate wedding accessories—they can play up the modern cut of a gown, add a flourish of romance against a lace veil, or pick up on the details in a tie and make a lapel pop.

Some couples will opt for tradition with color-coordinated florals across all bouquets and boutonnieres, which are elegant arrangements with complementary greenery. For others, it's a chance to make a statement with floral bouquets in colors and styles that represent each member of the wedding party's personality, in eye-catching hues pinned to fine suits, and with nonfloral family heirlooms or keepsakes to incorporate additional meaning.

PERENNIALLY POPULAR WEDDING FLOWERS

- Anemone
- Dahlia
- Hydrangea
- Lilac
- Orchid
- Peony
- Ranunculus
- Rose
- Sweet pea
- Tulip

ABOVE These color-coordinated accessories utilize different blooms—and the result is two very unique looks.

YOUR BOUQUET AND BOUTONNIERE STYLE

Flower selection can be overwhelming, even with the guidance of a trusted florist, wedding planner, and design team. Here's what to consider before you make your decisions.

- **TIME-TESTED AND TRUE** Popular perennial blooms like crisp roses, delicate baby's breath, and pretty peonies in single-hued bunches are romantic and timeless options that can complement any wedding style.
- **WHIMSICAL AND UNEXPECTED** Wildflowers full of character, bold mix-and-match colors and varieties, surprising tropical flower shapes, and quirky dried flowers and foliage are just a few options to make your florals pop.
- **GOING GREEN** Try personal foliage florals with fewer or no flowers. Popular greenery includes ferns, ivy, eucalyptus, and bay leaves.
- **FORGO FLORALS** For a fun twist, try a bouquet or boutonniere of feathers, origami flowers, branches of citrus, or other boutonniere alternatives like suit pins or badges.
- **TRY A POCKET BOUTONNIERE** In place of a pocket square and a separate pinned boutonniere, fill suit jacket pockets with small bouquets of flowers for a stylish alternative.

FROM TOP The same bouquet style for an entire wedding party creates a cohesive flow, especially when there's differing attire. • Bouquet shapes vary—opt for an organic cascade for a more whimsical look or a more geometric shape for a classic wedding.

A Bounty of Bouquets

Bouquets come in a few popular shapes and styles.

ROUND BOUQUETS

These bouquets feature flowers, often of the same bloom in the same color, bundled in a tidy, round shape that gives them their name.

CASCADING BOUQUETS

Almost like a waterfall of flowers, cascading bouquets have longer stems that spill over, trailing down the front of the arrangement.

BIEDERMEIER BOUQUETS

These interesting bouquets layer different blooms in a patterned circular design, creating a tightly structured arrangement.

HAND-TIED BOUQUETS

These bouquets are loosely tied together at the stems, giving them an unstructured appearance. They are often popular for rustic or boho weddings.

CLASSIC BOUTONNIERES
a single rose in a hue that matches the wedding's palette is a time-tested option.

ECLECTIC BOUTONNIERES
Skip flowers and use adornments like feathers, ribbon, broaches, and more for an unconventional statement.

5 THINGS TO KNOW WHEN CHOOSING YOUR BOUQUET AND BOUTONNIERE FLORALS

1. Your budget will guide your choices and priorities.

2. Seasonal availability helps determine costs, since in-season flowers will be more cost-conscious.

3. The color palette, style, and theme for your wedding's design, and even wedding party attire, will help your floral team recommend complementary flowers.

4. Flower meanings can assist you in choosing floral combinations that are more than just beautiful— they can express your joy and hope in a way that holds meaning to you.

5. If saving your blooms is important to you, consider preservation options with your florist in advance, since it might affect your selection.

PartySlate Tip

Go beyond the wedding party and recognize other important people at your celebration with corsages, bouquets, or boutonnieres. Grandparents will especially appreciate the comfort of wrist corsages over handheld options.

the reception

You're officially a couple. Let the celebrating—and eating, drinking, and dancing—begin! Here are the main design elements of the reception:

Tablescapes

A tablescape includes all the elements of your table that make up the full visual tableau. As with wedding styles, tablescapes come in a beautiful variety. They can be simple and understated, with one or two hues and a single texture, or a joyous explosion of playful colors, a thoughtful combination of dishware and glassware styles, and varying heights of votives, candlesticks, florals, and more. You can opt for one tablescape design throughout your reception, or can vary it from table to table.

Many venue packages include tablescape rentals such as tables, chairs, tablecloths, plates, flatware, and glassware. Venue rental items tend to be more basic, but you can work with your design team or an additional rental company to enhance those initial offerings with items that fit your wedding style.

With your design team, consider patterns, textures, and colors and how they interact with one another. There is no formula for creating the perfect tablescape, but adhering to your chosen color palette will create cohesion with the rest of your wedding's design. Choose one or two elements to stand out, and let the others play supporting roles.

THE ELEMENTS OF YOUR TABLESCAPE

Build your tablescape with these pieces—and anything else that inspires you!

- Candles
- Centerpieces
- Chargers
- Glassware
- Menus
- Napkins
- Plates
- Runners
- Silverware
- Tablecloths

Ask your wedding planner, venue, designer, or rental company for options of each element, then select complementary pieces that complete your full design.

THIS PAGE Create a layered look with linen, napkins, chargers, and menus in their own unique hues and patterns. • Off-the-table lighting sources add drama, especially when suspended at an outdoors wedding. **OPPOSITE** Candlelit tablescapes conjure romance and intimacy when the sun goes down.

INSPIRING CENTERPIECES

Consider these popular combinations:

- Colorful wildflowers and fresh citrus
- Hurricane-glass candleholders and single stems of flowers
- A single type of flower in a repeated design accompanied by simple votives
- Succulents, cacti, and fresh greenery
- Tapered candlesticks and lush floral arrangements in a rainbow of colors
- White florals, greenery, and wicker lanterns

ABOVE Bright, free-form floral centerpieces draw attention, while the pretty pastels and neutral tablecloth complement them. All the pieces work together.

Guerdy Abraira, lead event stylist for Guerdy Design and star of *The Real Housewives of Miami*, says that a "'Guerdyfy' party is always experiential; its tablescape design is no different." She recommends making your tablescapes meaningful by writing a note to each guest and putting it at their place setting "to truly make them feel special and seen."

CENTERPIECES

Abraira also suggests making sure that guests can see one another across the table without having to peek around centerpieces. "Ensure that low centerpieces are under chin level and high centerpieces are narrow in width from the top of the table and flare out only after it clears head level," she says.

Towering centerpieces make a statement, but low centerpieces allow for intimate conversation during a seated meal. Consider your priorities and what type of environment you want to facilitate for your guests. "When designing your wedding with your vendors, be sure to look up," Abraira says. "There may be some good hanging points where you can actually have florals, draping, or chandeliers set above your tablescape to create more of a wow experience."

When it comes to centerpieces, flowers are just the beginning. Cascading greenery, votives, tapered candlesticks, and even citrus and in-season produce can grace your reception tables.

ABOVE Bowls of citrus replace floral arrangements, and patterned linen and menus offer an added visual punch. The neutral wicker chargers and bamboo-handled flatware add tropical touches without pulling attention from the other details.

PLACE SETTINGS

Most venues include standard plates, glassware, and flatware in their packages, but don't hesitate to ask for other options. Place setting selections offer another chance to show some personality and tie into your wedding design. Mixed metal flatware, wine goblets in vibrant hues, scalloped or patterned plates, and decorative flatware can add interest and make your tablescape memorable.

LINEN AND DRAPING

Linen and draping complete a wedding reception design.

Linen is a décor element that can often be overlooked. But we believe that a table looks incomplete without the softening element of linen. Patterned tablecloths can serve as a focal point of your tablescape, while neutral-hued napkins can complement any design.

In addition to colors and patterns, there are also options like velvet, eyelet, lace, and more. And linen selection goes beyond tablecloths and napkins. Consider table runners (long strips of fabric that run down the center of a table), overlays (smaller cloths added over tablecloths, ending just past the lip of the table), and table skirts (fabric panels attached to the edge of tables to conceal their legs).

Choose from punchy patterns, different textures, and complementary colors—just be sure to consider your full tablescape when making your decisions. Believe it or not, elegantly mixing and matching patterned napkins and tablecloths could become one of the most memorable elements of your wedding design.

Draping may not be the star of your reception, but without it, your design may feel incomplete. Sheer drapery can transform your venue ceiling into a focal point, while drapery in bold hues can make a design statement and even divide your event space to fit your guest count.

PartySlate Tip

In-season flowers for your arrangements can be the most beautiful—and cost-effective. Work with your wedding planner and your florist to ensure your selections make sense for your season.

ABOVE Coordinate your tableware with your linen for a seamless look. An additional color in printed signage and backdrops makes them stand out. **OPPOSITE FROM LEFT** Paper butterflies bring a touch of bright whimsy to pastel tablescapes and gilded dinnerware. • Table linen in mint and sage add a light and airy feel paired with dreamy tented draping.

RENTALS

Many different décor elements fall into this very broad category. Rental items can be as grand as furniture vignettes and custom bars or as simple as glassware and silverware. You might opt for specialty rentals for every part of your wedding or mix statement rental pieces with your venue's offerings. You'll want to secure your rentals six months in advance.

Seating tends to be one of the most popular rentals. Most venues come with standard chair options, but couples can opt to rent styles that more closely match their wedding theme. For example, choosing ghost chairs can add a modern touch, while wicker seating creates a rustic feel.

Similarly, tables are another popular rental. When considering your options, think about table sizes and the experience you want your guests to have, since they'll spend much of the reception at their tables. Long tables offer a communal feel, while round tables facilitate conversation.

Another rental to consider is lounge seating. Adding groupings of sofas, armchairs, and tables throughout your reception space offers guests a dance floor break and a place to catch up with other guests.

PartySlate Tip

Custom rentals can be a perfect way to create a focal point for your reception. A floral-adorned stage, a custom bar complete with your monogram, or a lounge furniture vignette can add a special touch every couple is looking to incorporate.

YOU HAVE OPTIONS
Rentals to consider:

- Bar chairs
- Dance floors
- Décor elements, like vases and candleholders
- Dining tables
- Display tables
- Glassware
- High and low cocktail tables
- Installations, like custom backdrops and flooring
- Lounge furniture
- Linen
- Varied seating
- Serverware
- Silverware

Make a list of important elements, and work with your planner to identify who is providing which pieces.

THIS PAGE Chic rentals like these velvet armchairs in earthy hues elevate lounge groupings. • A sleek black bar feels both modern and minimalist with all-black glassware. **OPPOSITE** Delicate white umbrellas and neutral seating create a pleasing contrast with a lounge area in bold stripes and punchy citrus hues.

Print and Signage

Say it with signage. From highlighting the menu to explaining ceremony customs and details, signs guide your guests through each part of your celebration.

To make your signage distinctive, incorporate a logo designed for your event. Some couples love a monogram that blends their names or initials, while others prefer an illustration with special meaning. Also, think about cultural or religious symbols that are important to your heritage as a couple.

Make a list of everything you might want in a suite of materials before meeting with your vendor. Here are the most common options.

PartySlate Tip

It's all in the details, especially when it comes to printed materials for a wedding. Don't be afraid to get creative.

CEREMONY PROGRAMS

Programs are not necessarily a must-have when it comes to your printed items, but a program can enhance your ceremony. They inform guests about important customs, family members, and friends; they can include blessings or poems to be recited during the ceremony; and they help guests follow along with the event. Many couples also include a personal note within their ceremony program as a way to welcome guests to their celebration.

LEFT Carry your colorful blooms right onto you ceremony's programs for cohesion.

"I work in graphic design, so my wedding invitations were one of the most important elements to me. I learned not to underestimate the small details. From opting for raw edges that offered a vintage feel to leaning in to my romantic side with dusty rose ribbon, every decision we made in the process made a noticeable impact." —Megan, Michigan bride

SEATING ASSIGNMENTS AND FAVORS

Providing seating assignments for guests eases the flow of people into your reception space and removes guesswork. Place cards tend to be a more personalized option for communicating seating, but a seating chart can make a statement and serve as a design element for your reception. You can weave your wedding theme, season, or setting into seating assignments too.

If you're unsure about including a favor, consider combining your place cards and a favor in a single element. Mini succulents, cacti, or candles labeled with each guest's name and seating are some of our favorite options. We love when couples choose a gift that holds meaning, like a nod to the locale or a favorite food or drink.

FROM TOP Your place card wall should further your style, like this modern installation. • Pops of pink allium and fresh greenery with all-white place cards create a clean, summery look. • A bed of moss and floral-painted place cards create a beautiful garden aesthetic. • Here, multiple seating charts are framed by celestial blue hydrangea.

CLOCKWISE FROM TOP These Mediterranean-style plates pair perfectly with the custom menus in an analogous color scheme. • Handwritten ingredients are a picture-perfect way to showcase what's on the menu. • Consider adding illustrations to your custom menu designs.

PartySlate Tip

Don't forget to label your catering options. Most main courses will be accompanied by a menu, but passed items, late-night snacks, dessert tables, and buffets should also be labeled to help guide guests.

BELOW, FROM LEFT A mezcal tasting menu benefits from an earthy color palette and pressed vase with a few delicate blooms. • Custom cocktails add personality to bar offerings—as does this fun graphic menu. • Let the signature sips stand out with their own mini menu.

  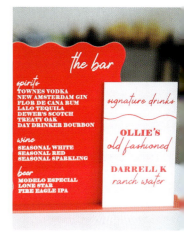

MENUS

Everyone knows that the eyes eat first, and that starts with the menu. We recommend placing a printed menu with each place setting, even if you're serving family style or at stations. This lets guests preview what's to come, and it also gets everyone excited as the meal progresses.

If you choose stations or a buffet, guests will appreciate additional menus near the food to help them navigate their options.

BAR SIGNAGE

Bar menus clearly—and creatively—set expectations with guests when it comes to your drink offerings. What types of liquor will guests have to choose from? Will the selections be limited to beer and wine? Will you offer specialty or signature cocktails? What about mocktails, seltzers, and soft drinks? In addition to providing information on your signs, you can add personal touches, like your monogram or images of your pets.

Questions to Ask Yourself

- ☐ What accommodations should your wedding team keep in mind for your guests in terms of mobility or seating during the wedding?

- ☐ What personal touches would you like to incorporate into your event design?

- ☐ Describe your ideal ceremonial focal point. What do you envision when you picture yourselves saying your vows?

- ☐ What kind of favors highlight your personalities or the theme and style of your event?

Questions to Ask Your Wedding Team

☐ Is seating provided by the venue? If so, does it align with our wedding vision?

☐ Is there a natural focal point in the venue that we should incorporate into the ceremony design?

☐ Can one ceremonial structure be repurposed during the reception?

☐ If cultural elements are important, how do we ensure they are integrated into our ceremony design?

☐ How can we repurpose the ceremony décor for the cocktail hour and reception?

☐ Are there ways to integrate special keepsakes or family heirlooms into the décor?

☐ How will our bouquets and boutonnieres stand out from those for our wedding party?

☐ How do we ensure that our tablescape encourages guest comfort and mingling while still wowing with design?

☐ What additional design and décor elements should we consider, like stage décor or tall arrangements?

☐ How can draping help separate the event space but also contribute to the ambiance?

☐ What printed elements should we consider, from programs to place cards?

☐ Should we consider rentals in addition to what our venue includes, like ghost chairs and colorful glassware?

SPEAK LIKE A PRO

arch a decorative structure used as a frame or support for ceremonies, often adorned with flowers, greenery, fabric, or other decorative elements

backdrop a decorative background or setting used as a focal point for ceremonies, receptions, or photo booths; may include draping, floral arrangements, signage, or other decorations

charger a decorative plate under the dinner plate as part of the place setting; they are larger than dinner plates and add elegance and visual interest to the table

lounge area a seating area at the reception or cocktail hour, typically furnished with sofas, chairs, and coffee tables for guests to relax and socialize

pipe and drape a structure that uses beautiful drapery to define and divide a space while adding color and texture

tablescape the all-encompassing design of your wedding tables, which might include place settings, linen, centerpieces, glassware, and table numbers

ABOVE Make sure your wedding team is knowledgeable in any cultural rituals that you will incorporate into your event.

chapter 6

Selecting Food & Drink

RIGHT Create a celebratory moment with a champagne tower. Swap the champagne for rosé or Aperol Spritz for a summery vibe.

PartySlate Tip

If your menu will be heavily influenced by local ingredients and seasonality, it's best to hold off on your tasting until closer to your wedding date so that you can try the actual dishes when they are freshly prepared.

ABOVE Turn your serving tray into a décor moment with curated shadow boxes. **RIGHT** Satiate and entertain guests at the same time with a course dedicated to molecular gastronomy.

Tastings

Any joyous occasion can be made even more wonderful by savoring an amazing meal with loved ones. Beyond providing your guests with nourishment so they can hit the dance floor, an amazing culinary experience is one of the most enjoyable—and talked about— moments of a wedding for your guests. They get to sit down, connect with one another, and celebrate you, all while being treated to a delicious meal in a beautiful setting. The first step in choosing what you serve and how you will serve it is sampling your caterers' suggested fare.

A tasting is your opportunity to try appetizer, entrée, and dessert options in advance. Your tasting will take place three to six months prior to your wedding date. Before your tasting, you will meet with your caterer to discuss preferences.

At your tasting, you will assess quality, flavors, presentation, and pairings. Your caterer may also present different presentation options and discuss any additional services available. Here are some tips for making your tasting go smoothly.

- **INVITE ALL KEY DECISION-MAKERS** For your tastings include your partner, planner, parents (if applicable), and so on.
- **TAKE NOTES** Keep track of the dishes and flavors you enjoy.
- **GIVE HONEST FEEDBACK** Talk to your caterer during the planning stages.
- **TALK WITH YOUR TEAM** Discuss food and beverage pairings as you sample them.
- **CONFIRM DETAILS** Don't forget dietary preferences, budgetary restrictions, service expectations, and cultural foods and traditions. (Read more at Food on page 114.)

Food

Selecting your menu is about more than just taste. You'll need to factor in:

- **BUDGET** When it comes to catering, that budget will be broken down into per-person costs.
- **FAVORITE FOODS** Are there any foods that are important to your relationship story? (Was your first date at an amazing pasta place, for example?) Are there any cultural or familial dishes you'd like to include?
- **GUEST REQUIREMENTS, RESTRICTIONS, AND ALLERGIES** Consider options for vegans, vegetarians, gluten-free diets, and other special dietary needs.
- **SEASONALITY** Fresh fare is always going to be the most flavorful and is often more eco-conscious.

You'll be able to share menu notes and tweaks based on flavors and presentation, as well as finalize types of service (how your food reaches guests—whether by servers, stations, carts), during your final tasting.

CLOCKWISE FROM TOP LEFT Opt for edible menus for a creative, photo-worthy bite. • Any dish can be made even more elegant through its presentation, including soup. • Extend personalization to cocktails with details like branded citrus. • Wow with a white cake by playing with shape and personalization. • Extend your monogram to tabletops for an extra wow factor. • Fare doesn't need to be fancy. Even burgers and fries can be presented beautifully. • Edible rings serve caviar with glamorous flair. • You can customize every detail—even the balsamic and olive oil bread dip—for a personal affair. • A unique lucite tray keeps service modern and memorable.

PARTY*SLATE*

114

WAYS TO WOW WITH CATERING

Cultural or familial nods Serve a dish made from your grandmother's recipe (with a menu note to explain its meaning) or that expresses a cultural tradition such as a challah cutting followed by a bread basket pass.

Interactive moments Offer live stations where guests can watch preparation and request customization for their preferences and dietary needs.

Presentation Think creative plating like soup poured tableside, synchronized service (with servers placing a course at every seat at a table simultaneously), edible spoons, and vintage glassware.

Service as entertainment Hire bartenders who can put on a show while they prepare creative cocktails—ask your cocktail caterer about the availability of flair bartending, in which bartenders flip or juggle bottles, or cocktail crafting demonstrations.

Surprise elements Opt for a cocktail that features aromatic smoke, set up a coffee cart, or offer bite-size desserts or a late-night snack delivered right to the dance floor.

make it yours

Personalize your fare with your monogram. It can be stenciled on food, piped onto cupcakes, or stamped into a delicious dessert.

Cocktail Hour

Generally the time between your ceremony and reception, cocktail hour serves as an important transitional moment during your event. It's the first time your guests can truly mingle and chat.

Where will you hold your cocktail hour? Since the space won't require seating for all guests, you can choose a more intimate spot within your venue. Is there a scenic space with a view, like a balcony or a terrace? Is there an ornate hall space, a bright and open catwalk, or a garden locale?

Next, think about how you want your cocktail hour to feel. Are you envisioning an elegant ambiance, with passed appetizers, a tall champagne tower, and a string quartet? Or do you picture guests gathering on cozy velvet lounge furniture under twinkling lights in a garden, toasting craft cocktails and filling plates from creative stations (like a hand-carved prosciutto display or pasta prepared in a Parmesan wheel)? Maybe you'd prefer a more relaxed vibe, with lawn games, local spirits, and fun food trucks? A memorable cocktail hour can reflect your individual personalities and shared interests.

ABOVE FROM LEFT Passed shucked oysters bring a classy casual vibe to an outdoor cocktail hour. • Miniature charcuterie boards add big flavor and adorable appeal. • Your cocktail tables are a main décor point, so prioritize chic linen rentals. **OPPOSITE** Leave plenty of room for mingling when choosing your cocktail hour event space.

PartySlate Tip

Remember to book entertainment for your cocktail hour. Music is important in creating your desired ambiance. You can also add interactive moments—for example, a roaming magician or mentalist, a fortune teller, a caricature artist, or a poet composing on-the-spot verses on a typewriter.

Service

Each popular service option offers opportunities for creativity and customization, and many couples opt for a mix of service styles at their wedding.

- **BUFFETS** Unveil these for any course—appetizers, dinner, or desserts. A buffet allows guests to choose from an appealing spread of options. Themed buffets are a fun twist on the usual. For example, represent different cuisines you love with dedicated stations, like a Thai noodle corner, a taco buffet, or a charcuterie spread.
- **CARTS** Roll out this fun delivery option for add-on non-main course foods like specialty desserts or coffee.
- **INTERACTIVE FOOD STATIONS** These offer next-level personalization—and even a bit of entertainment. From build-your-own taco bars or sundaes to live cooking stations, they add a dimension to your affair. Consider a sushi chef assembling custom maki or a paella station, with a chef tending to a massive carbon steel pan filled with savory rice and seafood.

OPPOSITE Server attire is a creative way to add color to your cocktail hour or reception.
BELOW, CLOCKWISE FROM TOP LEFT A live soup pouring makes service interactive. • Mini dutch ovens add a classic touch to any meal. • Live preparation merges entertainment and taste, like the Parmesan wheel pasta station.

- **TRAY-PASSED SERVICE** If you're looking for elegant yet convenient, this is perfect. Use it when you'd like guests to be up and mingling: upon arrival, at cocktail hour, and on the dance floor.
- **TABLE SERVICE** When you want guests to be seated and engaged with one another in intimate groups, this fills the bill (after all, you put a lot of thought into your table assignments). Table service can be plated or family style. Plated meals allow for artistic arrangements, perfectly composed flavors, and service with flair.
- **FAMILY-STYLE SERVICE** If you want to create a congenial vibe, have guests interact as they pass platters. It also lets guests portion their own meals.
- **THEMED STATIONS** Allow guests to pick and choose what they're interested in. Rather than one long buffet, each table station contains specific fare, such as a carving station for meats or a seafood station.

LEFT Colorful teas perched on glass shelves in translucent pots add a décor element all on thier own. **OPPOSITE, CLOCKWISE FROM TOP LEFT** Work with your rentals company to secure the right glassware for each cocktail. • Give a nod to your fur babies with custom stir sticks in your signature sips. • Try the time-tested combination of custom napkins paired with classic cocktails. • Tray-passed signature cocktails reduce bar lines and allow guests to keep mingling.

Drinks

In addition to standard bar offerings, consider these celebration-worthy sips.

- **SIGNATURE COCKTAILS** A signature drink reflects your tastes and personalities. Consider adding one or two to your menu. They could be your favorite drinks, sips that speak to your honeymoon, or curated drinks named after your pets.
- **A SPECIAL MOCKTAIL** Of course you'll have soda, tea, water, and more, but the next level in hospitality is to offer at least one nonalcoholic mixed drink that rivals the complexity and craft of the cocktails being offered.
- **ROAMING SIPS** Passed cocktails or table service can reduce crowds at the bar and allow more time for mingling.
- **CHAMPAGNE TOAST OR TOWER** Think about creating a moment that draws all your guests together, like a champagne toast or a champagne tower.
- **DRINKS WITH DESSERT** Consider digestifs, and serve coffee and tea. Elevate coffee service with a cart or trailer, an espresso machine, latte art, and mix-ins like flavored syrups, Baileys, and Kahlúa.

"Since we traveled for our destination wedding and couldn't bring our pup, Lincoln, we included him in details throughout the day. We added a hand-drawn illustration to cocktail stirrers, and the 'Lincoln's Libations' bar menus made our wedding even more special." —Kylie, *California bride*

Wedding Cakes and Desserts

The image of a towering tiered white cake is almost synonymous with weddings. But wedding desserts come in a fabulous variety of sugary options—including that cake. Increasingly, couples are offering a selection of sweets at their celebration such as:

- **DESSERT SPREADS** Full dessert spreads can complement or replace a couple's cake. Popular options include cupcakes, brownies, cookies, and more. Pie bars and crêpe stations are fun additions.
- **ONE-BITE TREATS** Passed treats like cake pops, doughnut holes, macarons, and mini Bundt cakes allow guests to enjoy sweets away from their seats (or even on the dance floor!).
- **THOUGHTFUL INCLUSIONS** Make sure you offer dessert options for guests with dietary restrictions. Lower-sugar options like fruit, as well as gluten- and dairy-free treats, are another way to be considerate of your friends and family.

PartySlate Tip

Cutting the wedding cake is always a highly photographed moment, so make sure yours is picture-perfect. Pressed flowers, loose petals, and more accents from your florist can make your wedding cake part of your décor.

CLOCKWISE FROM TOP LEFT A unique pleated design brings a modern twist to an all-white wedding cake. • Reimagine the tiered wedding cake with askew layers and geometric embellishments for a modern vibe. • Decadent florals add instant romance to any wedding cake and give the appearance of a watercolor painting. • Add pressed pansies and wildflowers to an all-white wedding cake for a whimsical treat.
OPPOSITE Create an interesting dessert cart with varied plated mini cakes in differing flavors and frostings. Oh, and don't forget the fresh florals.

Cake Considerations

If you do opt for a cake, the important factors are size (which will depend on guest count), flavor, and design.

CHOOSING YOUR FLAVORS

Have fun with your cake tastings, and sample to your sweet tooth's content. First, choose the base cake. Popular flavors include:

- Almond
- Carrot
- Chocolate
- Coconut
- Funfetti
- Lemon
- Marble
- Red velvet
- Strawberry
- Vanilla

Then choose frostings and fillings. Your baker will help you narrow down your options depending on your base and your favorite flavors. You may also opt to add in-season fruit. Don't be afraid to choose different flavors for each tier for a totally-you confection.

CAKE DESIGN

Your cake will be a focal point and will likely coordinate with your wedding décor. Its height, colors, and design offer opportunities for creativity. While white wedding cakes have a rich tradition, modern couples are choosing from an array of colors, with undulating frosting, metallic accents, real flowers, lighting, and more.

FROM TOP A simple monogram creates a photo-worthy cake. • Couples can swap florals for edible butterflies or other unique designs.

5 WAYS TO PERSONALIZE YOUR SWEETS

1. Opt for a custom cake topper with your names and likenesses or even figurines of your beloved pets.

2. Add your monogram to your desserts.

3. Ask your bakery to replicate your invitation liner or table-linen print on cookies or cupcakes.

4. Serve elevated takes on your childhood favorites, like Pop-Tarts or oatmeal cream pies.

5. Order a special treat from your home city or a cultural favorite.

LEFT Make your sips interactive with an ice sculpture cocktail chiller. Frozen roses add a romantic touch.

Questions to Ask Yourself

- ☐ What service options appeal to you for cocktail hour and reception dining?

- ☐ What are some of your favorite foods to enjoy together? How can you incorporate those into your meal service?

- ☐ What drinks do you, your family, or your friends particularly love?

- ☐ What personalization would you like to bring to your food and drink offerings?

- ☐ Are there any sweets special to you and your sweetheart? Any cultural desserts that speak to your family history? What flavors do you love? Describe your dream wedding dessert.

Questions to Ask Your Wedding Planner and Caterer

☐ Do you offer any seasonal specialty foods?

☐ Do you have any cultural specialties?

☐ How many people can join for the tasting?

☐ How many dishes can we sample?

☐ Can we incorporate our favorite dishes or ingredients into our menu?

☐ How do you accommodate guests' dietary restrictions and allergies?

☐ What surprising elements or displays can wow our guests?

☐ How many passed appetizers and stations do you recommend for cocktail hour?

☐ How many specialty cocktails and mocktails should we include in our bar service?

☐ Should we offer desserts in addition to or instead of our wedding cake?

SPEAK LIKE A PRO

buffet a style of meal service in which food is displayed on tables; self-service menus offer a variety of dishes to choose from

food pairings combining different flavors, textures, and ingredients to create a harmonious meal; may include wine pairings, cheese pairings, or combinations of savory and sweet flavors

food stations buffet-style setups in which different foods are served from separate stations; common choices include carving stations, pasta stations, taco bars, and dessert stations

hors d'oeuvres bite-size appetizers served before the main meal or during cocktail hour

passed appetizers small bites that are delivered to guests on trays by servers

service charge a fee added to the catering bill to cover the cost of staffing, setup, and other services provided by the caterer; typically a percentage of the total catering cost

stationary appetizers appetizers that are set up on station displays or platters; these may include cheese and charcuterie boards, fruit displays, and vegetable crudités

"One thing that was important to my fiancé, Mike, was ensuring that not only does the food look good but that it is easy to execute en masse. For example, a short rib is easier to keep warm than a fillet, which can easily dry out in heating boxes." —**Morgan,** *New Jersey bride*

BELOW Passed apps are the perfect opportunity to focus on local, quality ingredients, presented beautifully.

NOTES FOR MY WEDDING TEAM

MAKE LASTING MEMORIES

chapter 7

Creating Celebratory Moments

RIGHT Your wedding will be one of the most important days of your life, so plan at least one show-stopping moment during the celebration.

memorable moments

Your dream wedding is almost a reality. With your style and theme set, your venue and vendors booked, and your menu finalized, what's left to plan are the personalized moments that make your event special to you and your partner.

"While we, as designers, create extraordinarily beautiful environments, it's how we make the guests feel that they will recall for a lifetime," says Colin Cowie, chairman and CEO of Colin Cowie Lifestyle.

"I strive to include unique details that speak to the couple's DNA at all touchpoints," says Cowie. "From the moment guests receive the invitation—perhaps it includes a suite of custom illustrations related to the venue or the couple—to the time they depart—we may offer a 'newspaper' of the wedding weekend highlights and a scone for breakfast the next morning—I want to create meaningful connections so they'll always remember the emotions of that day with great fondness."

Schedule special moments throughout your day, from your ceremonial entrance to your exit at wedding's end, so that you and your guests will have sweet memories from your entire event.

....

ABOVE A great photographer won't just capture your joyful expressions, but also those of all of your friends and family celebrating your union.

PartySlate Tip

Couples often focus the majority of their wedding décor on the inside of the reception, but a grand entrance can leave your guests in awe. Candle-lined stairways and floral-framed doorways welcome your guests in style.

Capture the Special Moments

Here are 26 memorable moments from your wedding that you'll want photos of, so make sure they're highlighted in your day-of timeline for your photographer.

BEFORE YOUR CEREMONY

☐ Last casual moments with and without your wedding party

☐ Finishing touches, like donning a veil or cuff links

☐ First look with family or wedding party

☐ First look with partner

☐ Wedding arch photo shoot before guests arrive

☐ A pic with your pet if applicable

☐ Wedding party en route to ceremony

DURING YOUR CEREMONY

☐ Aisle before procession begins, with expectant faces turned

☐ Side-profile aisle shot as you walk toward the arch

☐ The ring exchange up close

☐ Your tiniest "off duty" attendants

☐ Meaningful cultural moments

☐ The ceremony, from above if possible

☐ Your kiss

☐ The "we did it" moment

DURING YOUR RECEPTION

☐ The decked-out reception space before it fills with guests

☐ All the little details you chose, from place cards and place settings to perfectly prepared custom cocktails and dishes

☐ The announcement of you and your partner as a married couple

☐ First dance (especially a dramatic dip)

☐ A photo taken from the stage out to the dance floor filled with your friends and family

☐ Any special performances or culturally significant moments

☐ Your reaction to sweet or funny speeches

☐ Guests raising their glasses

☐ Children enjoying the celebration

☐ Professional shots of groups taking selfies

☐ Your epic goodbye

PartySlate Tip

Let your most valued guests and photography team know in advance when these moments will take place, so that no one steps out at the wrong time. Your wedding planning team will also help ensure that your event is on schedule and that important parties are present for meaningful moments.

Entrances

It all starts with creating a wow-worthy entrance. "The entrance you design for your event acts as a glimpse into the soul of the party," says Jes Gordon, owner and creative director of jesGORDON | properFUN.

Nirjary Desai, chief experience officer of KIS(cubed) Events, adds, "The experiences of your celebration should be memorable, and when your guests walk into a space, your style should stand out to create the most unforgettable night they have ever attended."

Your big day includes several important entrances: your guests' entrance into your venue, you and/or your partner walking up the aisle to your ceremony, your guests' entrance into your reception, and your first entrance as a married couple. Creating a thoughtful entryway for each makes a lasting impression.

ABOVE You can personalize every element of your wedding, including your venue's facade. **RIGHT** Transform a straight path into a winding entryway with floral vignettes.

WOW-WORTHY ENTRANCE ELEMENTS

- Greenery tunnel
- Candles, lanterns, or chandeliers
- Cold fireworks
- Drapery
- Floral frames
- Lanterns
- Live performers
- Neon installations

ENTRYWAY DESIGN

A truly fabulous entry involves a bold décor moment that also flows seamlessly into the rest of your wedding. Start by working closely with your venue to use its best features to create grand entrances. For example, a stunning stairway can be flanked with florals and made a focal point for your entrance. Your venue's event team will also work with you to ensure any use of ceiling rigging, outside rentals, or live flames are within building code, so that everyone is safe.

Creative installations can multiply the wow factor exponentially—like a tunnel of flowers or a hallway bathed in hued lighting. You can use analogous colors or an ombré representation of your color scheme that is still harmonious with your design. If your reception design is floral forward, choose a different bloom in a similar shade or the same flowers in a bolder, brighter color to line your entrances.

Questions to Ask Yourself

☐ Guest entrances: What do you want them to see and hear as they enter your ceremony or reception space? Will attendants hand out any welcome items, programs, or favors?

☐ Your entrance into your ceremony: What do you want to see when you first enter your wedding ceremony space? Who will be with you? What do you want to see and hear as you walk up your aisle?

☐ Your entrance as a couple to your reception: Will you be announced? If so, how? What music should be playing, and how prominent should it be?

☐ Other entrances: Should there be announcements or special entrances for the hosts, wedding party, or guests of honor throughout your celebration?

Don't overlook the eco-and-budget-friendly option of repurposing your ceremony décor as a reception entrance element. Line a hallway with your aisle's florals, or define a doorway with your ceremonial arch.

Dance Floors and Dancing

Guests will gravitate to the dance floor thanks to your showstopping entertainment. But an eye-catching dance floor design can bring even the wallflowers toward the focal point of your reception space. Plus, it can draw the room together and makes for brilliant décor.

- **LOGISTICS** Your venue may not include a dance floor as part of its on-site rentals. For example, hotels are more likely to have dance floors, but historical venues and industrial spaces may require outsourcing. Even if your venue offers a dance floor, you may still want to bring in one for a different look and feel. Remember: Outsourced rentals will need to be delivered, assembled, broken down, and removed by an external vendor team.
- **GUEST COUNT** Your dance floor's dimensions should accommodate the number of guests at your reception. Some guests will abstain from dancing, and not everyone will be on the dance floor at the same time, but industry standards suggest allocating 4.5 square feet of space for each guest. It's also important to consider whether any cultural dances will require additional space.
- **CUSTOMIZATION** Your dance floor is another opportunity to bring in your wedding color palette or design motif, or you can personalize the space to tell your love story. For example, include your favorite quote, a map of where you met, or a print from your invitation's envelope liner. In addition to colors and patterns, dance floors come in varied materials and shapes. Imagine the vibe from a mirrored circular dance floor.

ABOVE A custom dance floor decal can complement your wedding florals.

WAYS TO CUSTOMIZE YOUR DANCE FLOOR

- Dance floor pattern washes and light projections
- Decal at the center of the floor
- LED lighting
- Monograms
- Projection mapping (see page 139)
- Suspended ceiling décor
- Distinctive materials, like tile
- Full-coverage wrap

CLOCKWISE FROM TOP A single design on an all-white dance floor results in a clean, crisp tableau. • A checkered black-and-white dance floor is always classic. • Dramatic florals can define a dance floor from above. • A ceiling installation of verdant greenery matching a botanical-print dance floor creates a secret garden feel. • A mix of table shapes and sizes—and a round dance floor—adds interest and variety.

SPECIAL DANCES

Throughout the reception, you may schedule special dances—with your partner or cherished guests—to important songs. These are meaningful moments that also break up the evening, entertain guests during food service, and honor relationships. Dances can be scheduled whenever you like throughout the night, but the first dance typically kicks off the reception. Here are some to consider.

- **FIRST DANCE** Whether it's a romantic slow dance or an exuberant choreographed beat, your first dance as a couple is a special moment to connect with your partner. It's also a perfect moment for your photographer to capture. To prevent distractions, shorten the original music if the song is long.

- **GUARDIANS' DANCE** This dance is a moment for you and your partner to focus on the special relationships with the people who raised you. Give your dance partners the chance to suggest music, and consider practicing beforehand to calm any nerves.

- **ANNIVERSARY DANCE** Honor the couples in attendance with an anniversary dance. Options include asking everyone married for a certain amount of time to take the floor, or simply ask the couple who has been together the longest to dance.

- **TRADITIONAL DANCES** Cultural dances like the hora, the sirtaki, and the money dance are delightful and meaningful ways to incorporate your personal and family history into your celebration and introduce your guests to your traditions.

PartySlate Tip

When choosing your first-dance song, consider lyrics, beat, dance style, timelessness, and meaning to your relationship.

Make It Your Own

Special dances we'd like to include:

_____

_____

_____

_____

_____

_____

_____

Songs that are important to us:

_____

_____

_____

_____

_____

_____

_____

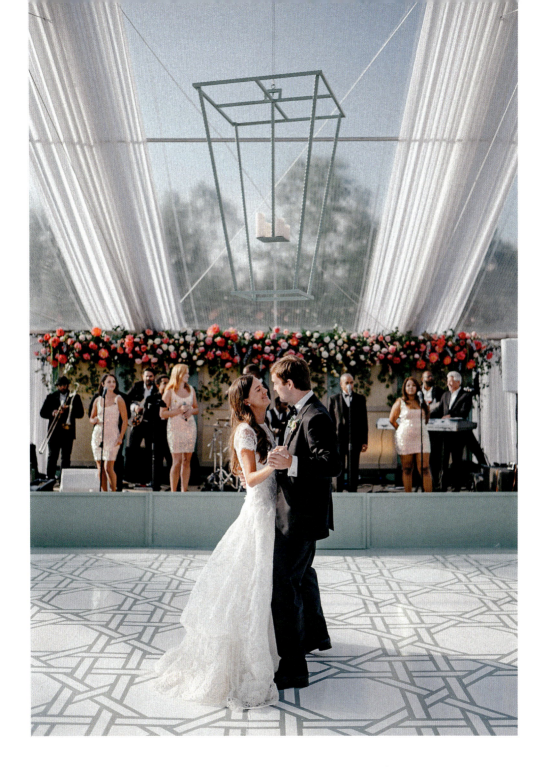

ABOVE Your first dance will be one the most cherished moments from your wedding celebration, so make sure the space is picture-perfect.

Lighting

Whether you surround your guests in the warmth of twinkle lights, drape your dining tables in the intimate glow of candlelight, or illuminate your dance floor with a burst of colored lights on the first beat of your favorite song, lighting affects the mood in every aspect of your event.

Using uplighting, pinspot lighting, projection mapping, and more can highlight individual decorative elements or the venue as a whole and create interactive and artistic elements. Lighting allows you to completely tailor the ambiance of your space, and it can easily double as décor. Candlelight beautifies tablescapes, but you can also use it to curate gorgeous backdrops, such as lining shelves with candles or using candles in hurricane glass to frame vignettes.

Blank walls become works of art with colorful uplighting or projections of geometric or botanical patterns. Suspended ceiling décor—twinkling string lights, lanterns, chandeliers, even floating candles suspended from the ceiling—add depth and texture to event spaces. Draped lighting creates intimate dining spaces within a larger venue or outdoor space.

And well-timed changes in lighting can also cue guests that your celebration is shifting—from cocktails to dinner, from dinner to dancing—or that an important moment is happening. Spotlights can focus attention on beloved rituals like cake cutting, speeches, or a first dance.

LIGHTING, DEFINED

Gobo lighting
Projection of a custom pattern or design onto walls, floors, or ceilings using a stencil-like device. For example, project your monogram for a personal touch or a leaf pattern to add even more lushness to a garden wedding dance floor.

Pinspot lighting
A concentrated beam of light that can make a big impact by highlighting a single element. For example, direct a pinspot light from the ceiling toward your wedding cake.

Projection mapping
A technique that projects moving images or video onto walls or other surfaces. For example, immerse guests in a forest of cherry blossoms to extend your design.

Uplighting
Lighting fixtures placed on the ground and aimed upward to illuminate walls, columns, or other architectural features. White or varied hues of light can enhance your palette and ambiance and create drama.

OPPOSITE, CLOCKWISE FROM TOP LEFT Sputnik chandeliers add even more glamour to a candlelit tablescape. • With the right installation, you can incorporate the chandelier of your choice into any outdoor reception. • Light your space high and low with glittering chandeliers and dreamy candlelight. • Custom neon signage provides both a swanky glow and a chic moment of personalization.

PARTYSLATE

MEMORABLE WEDDING EXIT IDEAS

Traditionally, wedding guests would toss rice as the couple left to wish them luck in their new life. Here are some modern twists so your loved ones can shower you with love as you wave farewell:

- Bubbles
- Confetti
- Flower petals
- Glow sticks
- Pom-poms
- Sparklers
- Streamers

Speeches

Every moment of your wedding day will be important, but years from now, you'll surely remember sentimental moments like toasts and cultural traditions.

When it comes to speeches, many couples opt to keep their wedding program short and sweet so their guests stay engaged. You can also spread out toasts throughout the weekend, giving your most important guests the chance to stand up and say a few words.

Exits

Your wedding exit is your farewell to your guests. It's their last glimpse of you before you set out on your new adventure as a married couple. It will also be the final moment of your wedding, so imbue it with meaning and the right amount of pomp.

ABOVE Your wedding exit is a chance to get playful. **RIGHT** Speeches are easily one of the most meaningful parts of any reception, so consider hiring a videographer to capture these moments.

Whether you choose a classic send-off or a one-of-a-kind exit, distinguish this final moment from all the others that came before it.

The best wedding exits allow for guest participation. Give your friends and family something to hold or toss as they celebrate you and your spouse one last time. An epic exit also makes for brilliant photo ops. Heighten the drama by adding fireworks or live musicians or driving away in a vintage car. Personalize it by including your pet as an escort or having your guests wave pom-poms in your alma mater's colors.

PartySlate Tip

Make sure your photographer is there to capture your final wedding moment. Many photographers are available for only a certain number of hours, so schedule your priority moments with them in advance.

Questions to Ask Your Designer and Planner

☐ Should we create a custom dance floor or use the one our venue offers?

☐ If we have a monogram, where can we incorporate it throughout our celebration?

☐ When should special dances with parents or family members take place during the reception?

☐ What type of lighting will elevate my wedding décor?

☐ If we have a cultural dance we want to include, when will that take place?

☐ If we want to make a grand exit, what options do you recommend?

☐ Who should give speeches, and at what point during the wedding weekend?

SPEAK LIKE A PRO

LED dance floor a dance floor with built-in LED lights that can change colors, patterns, and effects, creating a dynamic and visually striking atmosphere for dancing

scheduling your day an hour-by-hour breakdown of what should happen on your wedding day; develop it with your partner, your planner, and your wedding team

shot list a list you will make to inform your photographer of the different combinations of guests or timing of important moments you want captured

wrap or decal a piece of adhesive, typically made out of vinyl, that adheres to a dance floor, a bar, steps, or another area to customize its design

---

NOTES FOR MY WEDDING TEAM

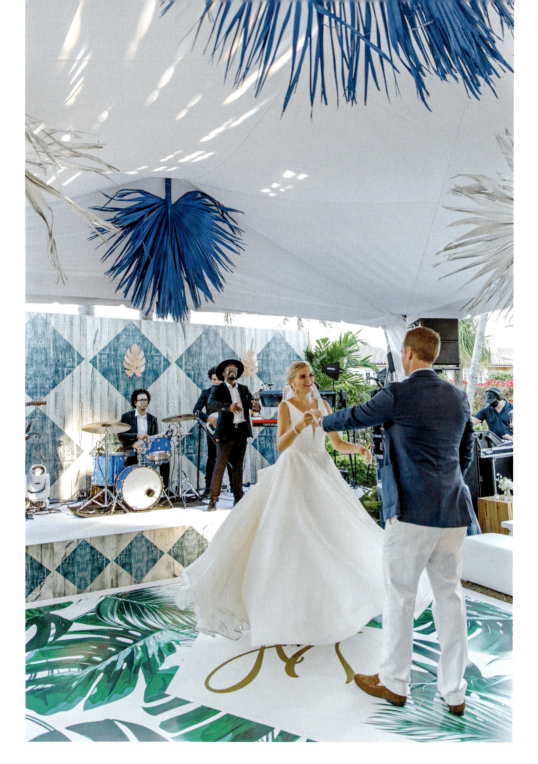

ABOVE Mix and match décor elements in a defined palette for an eclectic celebration.

chapter 8

Engaging Guests

RIGHT Celebrate your love with a show-stopping performance on a beautifully decorated stage.

the party

Great party entertainment helps guests remember how they *felt* during an event—and that's not limited to your band or DJ keeping your reception lively. Thoughtful entertainment throughout your big day will keep guests engaged and set the tone for each moment of your celebration. Here's some inspiration for entertainment moments throughout your wedding.

Ceremony

Personalizing your nuptials with special entertainment can make them even more memorable. Choose entertainment for the moments you most want to emphasize, such as:

- Harpists or a string quartet playing as guests arrive and sit down
- Ballerinas dancing down the aisle before the wedding processional
- A live singer performing as each member of the wedding party walks up the aisle
- A gospel choir erupting in song as you and your partner kiss and then leading the wedding recessional

LEFT Instead of a stage, opt for ground-level floral décor to create a designated space for ceremonial entertainment.

PartySlate Tip

Work with your entertainment team to plan a walk to remember from your cocktail hour to your reception or from your reception to the after-party. A fun-filled parade is a festive and memorable way to get from here to there.

FROM TOP Transport guests from one part of your celebration to the next with memorable entertainment. • A vintage rotary phone audio guest book doubles as a chic photo op.

Cocktail Hour

Because your cocktail hour is a transitional time and an important moment for your friends and family to mix and mingle, soft background music that engages but doesn't distract is a great way to create ambiance. That can be live, in the form of a string quartet or a singer-guitarist, or cued up by an experienced DJ. Cocktail hour is also an opportunity for personalization; for example, you could add:

- A live poet who writes custom odes to guests
- Cocktail napkins with fun facts about the couple to act as a conversation starter
- An opportunity for guests to leave messages for the couple, whether in a guest book or by recording a video message

Reception

Music sets the tone for your reception, so spend time building your perfect playlist with your band or DJ. Specialty entertainment can round out your event. Here are some ideas to inspire you.

- A painter capturing the scene in real time
- An aerialist or other circus-type act
- A showstopping dance performance
- A surprise performance by a celebrity or an entertainer
- Fireworks set to music
- A live champagne or cocktail tower pour
- Synchronized swimmers if your venue has a pool
- A hand-rolled-cigar bar

ABOVE An experienced wedding entertainment company will lure all guests to the dance floor, even the wallflowers. **OPPOSITE, CLOCKWISE FROM TOP LEFT** An electric violin adds an element of intrigue to your entertainment hour. • A flexible wedding band can get right down to the dance floor and mingle with guests as they perform. • If your venue has a pool, consider synchronized swimmers for a performance that will wow your guests. • Curate an intimate moment with a solo performance.

ABOVE Consider unique interactive entertainment, like this second line parade in New Orleans. **BELOW** If hosting a destination wedding, opt to incorporate local entertainment traditions into your celebration. **OPPOSITE** Even traditional weddings can benefit from a playful photo booth.

Another way to add fun flourishes and get family and friends involved in special moments is with cultural, religious, and geographical customs. For example, a Nigerian wedding might feature a spray that showers the dance floor with money and is often accompanied by Afrobeat. An Irish wedding could incorporate bagpipe performers, while a wedding in New Orleans is likely to host a second-line parade that everyone can join. Whatever your location or traditions, make sure you secure any specialty performers you will need to make the moment special.

Also, work with your planner to incorporate these traditions into your wedding timeline so that your guests (and photographer) don't miss a moment.

SAY CHEESE

One of the most popular wedding entertainment options is a photo booth—and your choices are seemingly endless.

360-degree booth
A camera that swings in a full circle around guests perched on a platform to record short, shareable video clips.

Classic photo booth
A stationary spot with a custom backdrop and fun props that engage guests who receive a printed photo strip, an image, or electronic files for sharing.

Mobile booth
A roaming photographer captures friends and family on the dance floor, at the bar, and elsewhere. Then they apply a custom virtual frame and share the album digitally with partygoers.

After-Party

Don't want the fun to stop? An after-party carries the revelry of your wedding beyond the last reception dance. It is a less formal gathering, often in a nearby space, that keeps the party going. Upbeat tunes are imperative. Many couples who opt for a live band for their reception switch to a DJ for their after-party. You can even consider a karaoke setup.

You'll also want to make sure your after-party has a dance floor, moody lighting, and your favorite late-night bites (like doughnuts, pizza, and sliders). Get creative with a theme that expresses your personality. If you met in college, use your school colors in your décor. Serve food and cocktails inspired by your honeymoon.

PartySlate Tip

Whether you opt for a band or a DJ, you'll want to extend your photographer and videographer into the after-party for the most candid, relaxed, and silly moments of your wedding.

Questions to Ask Yourself

☐ In what ways do you want to personalize your ceremony?

☐ What special moments would you like to occur during your cocktail hour?

☐ What special moments would you like to occur during your reception? Think speeches, cultural traditions, special stations, and delightful surprises.

ABOVE Let your guests know that the after-party has officially started with bold, custom signage. **OPPOSITE FROM LEFT** Turn your late-night bites into a cute photo op with the right attire. • Bring out the confetti and glow sticks for a memorable after-party.

Questions to Ask Your Wedding Planner and Entertainment Company

☐ What type of entertainment is best for each part of our wedding: ceremony, cocktail hour, reception, after-party?

☐ How many songs should we select for the ceremony processional and recessional?

☐ What creative entertainment ideas can we add to our cocktail hour to engage guests?

☐ Other than music, what types of entertainment do you suggest for the reception?

☐ What types of entertainment can we incorporate that are culturally significant to us?

☐ What are the different types of photo booths, and which do you recommend?

SPEAK LIKE A PRO

insurance some venues require proof of insurance from vendors like bands and DJs

rider a document outlining a band's requirements, including technical specifications, equipment, and any additional needs (like dressing rooms or meals)

set list the list of songs a band or a DJ plans to perform or play; you can make special requests, including songs you don't want included

NOTES FOR MY WEDDING TEAM

ABOVE A cold fireworks display draws all eyes to a special moment.

chapter 9

Arranging Weekend Events

RIGHT Linen and florals aren't where
pops of color begin and end; we love the fresh citrus
at each setting at this chic wedding.

Wedding-Related Events

Your wedding can span more than one day. In fact, many modern couples opt for a weekend of celebrations, especially for guests who traveled for the occasion. Use every minute of your weekend to bring guests together and revel in all the love.

"Events surrounding your wedding provide additional opportunities to spend time with the people you love—and for them to connect and get to know each other," says Michelle Norwood, founder and CEO of Michelle Norwood Events. "I like to recommend a prewedding event, such as a welcome party or a rehearsal dinner, and a postwedding gathering, like a brunch or daytime activity—especially if you have friends and family traveling for your wedding. Your nuptials and reception will fly by, and it will be hard to spend quality time with everyone during the main event."

WELCOME PARTY

Welcome-party invites are typically extended to your entire guest list. They set the tone for the weekend. They are more relaxed affairs than your wedding, so you can incorporate ideas you would not with a more formal event. Consider a theme inspired by your locale, how you met, things you love to do together, or anything else meaningful to you.

ABOVE Destination weddings often feature multi-day events, so make sure to budget for a photographer from start to finish. **OPPOSITE, CLOCKWISE FROM TOP LEFT** Thank guests with thoughtful welcome baskets—and the perfect selfie backdrop. • Weekend events offer the opportunity to be playful with your cocktails. • Distinguish your rehearsal dinner with unique details like this monogrammed serving linen. • Give your welcome gifts a theme for an extra thoughtful presentation.

PartySlate Tip

Remember, the rehearsal dinner is an opportunity to spend quality time with loved ones and to thank them for their support and participation in the wedding itself. Your rehearsal dinner is a great time for you and your partner to toast your wedding party and participants and give them gifts if you plan to do that.

REHEARSAL DINNER

Rehearsal dinners serve two purposes: They reserve time for you and your wedding party to, well, rehearse, and it's a fantastic time for family and close friends to connect before the hubbub of the big day. Similar to a welcome party, you also get time to mix and mingle with those closest to you and your partner.

Rehearsal dinners are typically reserved for anyone in the wedding party, anyone who has a role in the ceremony or reception, and immediate family members. Depending on who is hosting the dinner and what the budget is, the invitation may be extended to other close friends and family members. Let your rehearsal dinner be a time to slow down and bask in all the love and support of your closest people.

OPPOSITE AND ABOVE A welcome party is the perfect time to let your creativity run wild. Opt for colorful attire to match your vivid welcome party décor.

ACTIVITIES

Prearranged activities are a great way to get your guests excited for the weekend, especially for destination weddings. Traveling to a new locale can be costly for guests, and bundling activities into your weekend's itinerary takes the pressure off them to make arrangements for themselves. Group activities are also a great way to make memories with your loved ones throughout the weekend and help them connect with one another in more natural and casual settings than the wedding itself.

THIS PAGE Add local color and experiences to your wedding weekend itinerary. • Think outside of the limo and provide fun modes of transportation to wedding weekend events.

Questions to Ask Yourself

Which wedding weekend activities are you interested in providing for guests? To help you book the events and execute your plan, make notes for your wedding team in the space provided.

☐ Activities for children
☐ Sightseeing tours
☐ Guided nature walks
☐ Dinner at a restaurant
☐ Farewell brunch

☐ Gather at a bar
☐ Group exercise sessions
☐ Picnic
☐ Religious ceremonies
☐ Spa day

Other ideas
_____
_____
_____
_____

PARTY*SLATE*

162

FAREWELL BRUNCH

The farewell brunch means your weekend is coming to a close, but it's still an event to look forward to. Says planner Michelle Norwood, "A day-after event offers the added benefit of getting to hear all of your guests' stories from your wedding, allowing you to relive the highlights right away."

Part of the fun of hosting a wedding is knowing your guests had the best time—and hearing all about it.

ABOVE Your guests (and you) will likely be tired after such a lively weekend, so make sure to offer plenty of refreshments and some last moments at your farewell brunch.

Don't feel restricted to a formal brunch. Depending on your wedding locale, you could opt for a pool party, a morning at a vineyard, or even a day at the beach. Be inspired by your wedding destination, and prioritize fun!

PartySlate Tip

Request RSVPs for your farewell event with your wedding invitation replies so you know how many people to expect and budget for (many will travel home after the reception).

Questions to Ask
Your Wedding Planner

☐ Do we need a welcome party
and a rehearsal dinner?
If yes, what is the difference
between the two?

☐ Who should be invited to each
of the weekend events?

☐ Does a rehearsal dinner have to
be a sit-down dinner, or can it
be a more casual affair?

☐ What types of creative activities
can we incorporate into our
wedding weekend events to
make them memorable?

NOTES FOR MY WEDDING TEAM

ABOVE The intimacy of pre- and post-wedding events lend themselves to gorgeous tablescapes that facilitate heartfelt conversations.

chapter 10

Tackling To Dos After the Party

RIGHT Make your wedding exit as exciting
and memorable as your entrance.

Postwedding Tasks

As you revel in the afterglow of your wedding experience, there are still a few items to finish. Postwedding tasks are essential to ensure a smooth transition to married life and to wrap up any loose ends from your celebration. Amrit Dhillon-Bains, owner and planner with Anais Events, says, "We create a personalized timeline with a to-do list for postwedding tasks based on etiquette, the couple's priorities, and the flexibility of their own schedules. For instance, dresses should be sent for preservation immediately to prevent stains and damage from setting in. Thank-you notes can be sent out as soon as possible while the memories are fresh, often within two to three months. For photo albums, some couples could start planning varied books for each side of the family early but will have to wait until the photos come in from the photographer; generally it's common to complete the album within six to 12 months of the wedding."

Here is a list of common postwedding tasks and when to do them.

AS SOON AS POSSIBLE

☐ Return rental items, like tuxedos and jewelry.
☐ Preserve wedding attire. Have your wedding dress and other attire professionally cleaned and preserved.
☐ Unpack and organize wedding gifts.
☐ Write down a list of gifts, and gather addresses.

WITHIN A FEW MONTHS

☐ Complete thank-you cards. Thank family and friends for their attendance and gifts, and don't forget to thank vendors.
☐ Return or exchange duplicate and unwanted gifts.
☐ Pay final vendor balances, plus gratuity. Complete vendor reviews.

WITHIN A YEAR

☐ Collect and review wedding photos and videos. Work with your wedding photographer to preserve them in an album.
☐ Close or update your wedding registry (guests have up to one year to send a gift, so don't rush on this one).
☐ Create a memory box or scrapbook to store keepsakes, including invitations, programs, and special photos.

LEFT Work with your photographer to choose your favorite images to share, create an album, or frame. This tree-lined image is surely a favorite. OPPOSITE Your big day is all about you and your beloved, so make sure to lean into your own unique style—and choose a vendor team that can bring your vision to life.

final words

You have everything you need to create the wedding of your dreams. Remember to appreciate all the moments, from the planning and try-ons all the way through to the farewells and thank-yous. Your wedding is just the beginning. What follows is a beautiful life with your partner. Congratulations.

photo credits

NOTE All photography credits are listed clockwise from top left

· ·

COVER Photographer: KT Merry Photography; **Planner:** Mindy Weiss Party Consultants; **Floral Design:** Jeff Leatham; **Design, Décor & Draping:** Revelry Event Designers; **Rentals:** Casa De Perrin; **Lighting:** Images By Lighting; **Candles:** Vogue Candles

PAGE 1 Photographer: O'Malley Photographers; **Planner:** Callista & Company; **Florals:** Wild Bloom by Kristen Griffith-VanderYacht; **Venue:** Cave B Estate Winery

PAGE 2 Photographer: Nico Leon; **Planner & Designer:** Victoria Dubin Events; **Art Direction & Florals:** Ed Libby Events; **Lighting:** Fusion Productions; **Furniture Rentals:** HIGHSTYLE Event; **Linen:** Nuage Designs

PAGE 5 Photographer: John & Joseph Photography; **Planner:** Mindy Weiss Party Consultants; **Florals:** Mark's Garden; **Venue:** Four Seasons Los Angeles at Beverly Hills

PAGE 6 Photographer: Valorie Darling Photography; **Planner:** Nicole Alexandra Events & Designs; **Design & Florals:** Butterfly Floral & Event Design; **Venue:** La Quinta Resort & Club; **Lighting:** Amber Event Production

PAGE 9 Photographer: Michelle Beller Photography; **Planner:** Details Event Planning; **Floral Design:** Mark's Garden; **Décor:** Revelry Event Designers

PAGE 10 Photographer: Katie Edwards Photo; **Planner & Designer:** Kristin Banta Events; **Rentals:** Collective Rentals; **Venue:** Carmel Valley Ranch

PAGE 11 Photographer: Mari Harsan Studios; **Planner:** A Fine Fête; **Florals:** Love Blooms; **Rentals:** Something Vintage Rentals, Select Event Group

PAGE 12 Photographer: Carter Rose Weddings; **Planner:** Alison Baker Events; **Décor & Florals:** Three Branches Floral Design; **Venue:** Park Hyatt Beaver Creek Resort & Spa; **Tent:** Stage Works, Sandone

PAGE 13 Photographer: Caroline Jurgensen Photography; **Planner:** Caroline Events; **Florals:** Gro Designs •

Photographer: Jessica Bordner Photography; **Planner & Invitations:** Posh Parties; **Floral Design:** Xquisite Events

PAGE 14 Photographer: Anya Kernes Photography; **Planner:** Callista & Company; **Florals:** Max Owens Design; **Décor & Lighting:** JD Events; **Venue:** Borgo Finocchieto

PAGE 16 & 17 Photographer: Clane Gessel Photography; **Planner:** Sonal J. Shah Event Consultants; **Décor:** Design House Decor; **Venue:** Hyatt Regency Jersey City; **Stationery & Graphics:** Emily Kathryn Paper; **Lighting:** Bentley Meeker Lighting & Staging, Inc.

PAGE 18 Photographer: Valorie Darling Photography; **Planner:** The Lynden Lane Company; **Florals:** Keith J. Laverty; **Stationery & Calligraphy** Katie O'Brien; **Linen:** La Tavola Fine Linen; **Custom Décor:** EDGE Design and Decor; **Tabletop:** Casa De Perrin; **Lighting & Draping:** Amber Event Production; **Venue:** Newport Beach Country Club

PAGE 19 Photographer: Abby Jiu Photography; **Planner:** Lauryn Prattes Styling and Events; **Design & Florals:** Birch Event Design; **Venue:** The Hay-Adams

PAGE 20 Photographer: Brett Hickman Photography; **Planner:** Blissfully Styled Events; **Design & Florals:** Beautiful Savage Flowers; **Venue:** Rancho Las Lomas; **Stationery:** Jen Simpson Design; **Table Numbers:** Ultimate Design

PAGE 21 Photographer: Shawn Connell Weddings; **Planner:** Pejy Kash Events; **Florals:** Ivie Joy Floral Arts; **Rentals:** Glam Party Rentals, Taylor Creative Inc., Westside Party Rentals; **Lighting:** Geo Events Design

PAGE 22 Photographer: Matt Rice Photography; **Planner:** Posh Parties; **Design, Décor & Florals:** Renny & Reed; **Venue:** Faena Hotel Miami Beach

PAGE 23 Photographer: Corbin Gurkin; **Planner:** Bruce Russell Events; **Indian Event Design:** The Wedding Design Company; **Florals:** Amie Bone Flowers; **Caterer & Florals:** McCalls Catering & Events; **Production & Rentals:** Hensley Event Resources

PAGE 24 Photographer: Rachel Havel Photography; **Planner & Designer:**

GoBella Design & Planning; **Décor & Florals:** Siloh Floral; **Venue:** The Little Nell

PAGE 26 Photographer: Duke Images; **Planner:** Colin Cowie Lifestyle; **Florals:** Aria Vera Floral; **Venue:** Chileno Bay Resort

PAGE 27 Photographer: Jess Onesto; **Planner:** Madix & Co.; **Florals:** Rust & Flourish; **Venue:** Viansa Winery; **Rentals:** Encore Events Rentals

PAGES 28 & 29 Photographer: Stetten Wilson; **Planner & Designer:** Amorology; **Florals:** Native Poppy; **Venue:** Park Hyatt Aviara Resort; **Rentals:** The Hostess Haven, borrowed BLU, Folklore Rentals; **Linen:** BBJ La Tavola, Nuage Designs; **Calligraphy:** Four Things Paper

PAGE 30 Photographer: Rachel Havel Photography; **Planner:** Keely Thorne Events; **Florals:** Bows and Arrows Flowers; **Venue:** T-Lazy-7 Ranch

PAGE 31 Photographer: Tamara Gruner Photography; **Planner:** NSWE Events; **Florals:** Life In Bloom; **Venue:** Milwaukee Country Club; **Tent:** Blue Peak Tents

PAGE 32 Photographer: Abby Jiu Photography; **Planner & Designer:** ROQUE Events; **Florals:** Flower Girl Em; **Venue:** Four Seasons Resort and Residences Napa Valley; **Rentals:** Found Rental Co., Theoni Collection, La Tavola Fine Linen

PAGE 33 Photographer: John & Joseph Photography; **Planner:** Ashley Chanel Events; **Venue:** Roblar Winery

PAGE 34 Photographer: Niki Marie Photography; **Planner:** Elegant Occasions by JoAnn Gregoli; **Florals:** Peonies to Paint Chips

PAGE 35 Photographer: Matt Rice Photography; **Planner:** Posh Parties; **Design, Décor & Florals:** Renny & Reed; **Venue:** Faena Hotel Miami Beach; **Escort Cards:** Calligraphy Chik

PAGE 36 Photographer: Hunter Ryan Photo; **Planner:** Carrie Darling Events; **Florals:** Kaleidoscope Floral

PAGE 39 Photographer: Yarin Darshan; **Planner & Designer:** Tal Orion Conceptual Events; **Florals:** Renaissance Flowers Plus; **Venue:** Hummingbird Nest Ranch

PARTYSLATE

PAGE 40 Photographer: Chard Photo; Planner & Designer: Emily Clarke Events; Florals: Pina Cate; Venue: Zadun Reserve

PAGE 42 Photographer: Niki Marie Photography; Planner: Shannon Gail Events; Décor & Florals: Revel Decor; Venue: Four Seasons Hotel Chicago; Linen: BBJ La Tavola • Photographer: Carter Rose Weddings; Planner: Kelly Karli Weddings & Events; Florals: Olive & Poppy • Photographer: Apollo Fotografie; Planner: Cultural Event Rentals; Florals: Nicole Ha Floral Design

PAGE 44 Photographer: Jose Villa; Planner: Easton Events; Décor & Florals: IAMFLOWER; Venue: Amanpuri

PAGE 45 Photographer: KT Merry Photography; Planner & Designer: Daughter of Design; Planner: PLANNIE • Photographer: Scott Clark Photo; Planner & Designer: Neon River Weddings; Floral: Designs by Ahn • Photographer: ein photography and design; Planner: LLG Events; Florals: Bardin Palomo; Venue: Tribeca Rooftop

PAGE 46 Photographer: Apollo Fotografie; Planner: B Beloved Events; Décor: R&R Event Rentals; Florals: Flowers By Edgar, Enchantment Floral

PAGE 49 Photographer: Niki Marie Photography; Planner: Shannon Gail Events; Venue: Four Seasons Hotel Chicago

PAGE 51 Photographer: Rudney Novaes Photography; Planner, Design & Florals: Kesh Events; Venue: Oheka Castle

PAGE 52 Photographer: Roey Yohai Studios; Planner & Designer: Victoria Dubin Events; Design & Florals: Ed Libby Events, Venue: Cedar Lakes Estate

PAGE 53 Photographer: LAUREN + ABBY ROSS; Planner: Michelle Rago Destinations • Photographer: Nico Leon; Planner: jesGORDON | properFUN • Photographer: Harwell Photography; Planner: TOAST events; Florals: Edge Design Group; Venue: Four Seasons Hotel Atlanta • Photographer: Natalie Watson Photography; Planner, Design & Florals: Bliss Events Chicago; Venue: The Old Post Office; Linen: Nuage Designs; Lighting: Frost Chicago

PAGE 54 Photographer: LA76 Strategic Design; Planner & Designer: Rafanelli Events; Venue: Viceroy Los Cabos

PAGE 55 Photographer: Rene Zadori; Planner: Mary Michelle; Florals: Dolce Fiore; Venue: Hummingbird Nest Ranch; Rentals: Premiere Party Rents

PAGE 56 Photographer: Vicki Grafton Photography; Planner & Designer: Pamela Barefoot Events + Design; Florals: Sophie Felts Floral Design; Venue: Whitehall • Photographer: Nate Shepard Photo; Planner: Table 6 Productions–Colorado; Florals: Wildflowers Events and Occasions; Venue: The Abaco Club on Winding Bay

PAGE 57 Photographer: Eric Kelley Photography; Planner & Designer: Easton Events; Florals: Sarah Winward; Venue: Amangiri

PAGE 58 Photographer: Sergio Sandoná Photography; Planner: Jennifer Zabinski Events; Design: Rodrigo Mora • Photographer: Roey Yohai Studios; Planner: Leslie Mastin Events; Design & Florals: David Beahm Experiences; Venue: 620 Loft & Garden; Rentals: Party Rental Ltd.; Linen: Napa Valley Linens

PAGE 59 Photographer: KT Merry Photography; Planner & Designer: Easton Events; Florals: Kathleen Deery Design; Venue: Black Swan Lake; Tent: Skyline Tenting • Photographer: Katie Kett Photography; Planner: Celebrate Event Planning & Design; Design & Florals: Yanni Design Studio; Venue: The Rookery

PAGE 61 Photographer: READYLUCK; Planner: ASE, Amanda Savory Events; Design: Little Sister Creative; Venue: The Bordone LIC

PAGE 63 Photographer: Callaway Gable; Planner: Alyson Fox - Alyson Fox Events; Florals: Mark's Garden; Design: Revelry Event Designers; Venue: Four Seasons Hotel Westlake Village; Lighting: Images By Lighting

PAGE 65 Photographer: Abby Jiu Photography; Planner: Simply Chic Events; Venue: Pippin Hill Farm & Vineyards; Rentals: STRADLEY DAVIDSON

PAGE 66 Photographer: Duke Images; Design: Stacy Porras Wedding Consulting; Florals: Butterfly Floral & Event Design; Venue: Terranea Resort

PAGE 67 Photographer: Towards The Moon; Planner: Pejy Kash Events; Florals: Ivie Joy Floral Arts

PAGE 68 Photographer: Logan Cole Photography; Planner & Designer: Nicole Alexandra Events & Designs; Live Painter: Lisa Owen

PAGE 69 Photographer: Anna Shackleford; Planner: Mariée Ami; Design & Florals: Jackson Durham Events; Entertainment: Matt Thelen Entertainment, The River Town Band; Venue: Montage Palmetto Bluff

PAGE 70 Photographer: Michael Jurick Photography; Planner: Untouchable Events; Design: Anthony Taccetta Event Design; Caterer: Marcia Selden Catering & Events

PAGE 71 Photographer: Shea Christine Photography; Planner: Masi Events; Production & Florals: Renny & Reed; Venue: The Breakers Palm Beach

PAGE 72 Photographer: du soleil photographie; Planner: Fulton Events; Stationery: Paper Betty

PAGE 73 Photographer: Perry Vaile; Planner: Eva Clark Events; Design & Florals: Floressence Flowers; Venue: Mountaintop Golf & Lake Club; Stationery: Dear Elouise

PAGE 74 Photographer: KT Merry Photography; Planner & Designer: Masi Events; Florals: Parrish Designs of London; Paper Goods: Fin Fellowes • Photographer: Todd James Photography; Planner & Designer: Emily Coyne Events; Florals: Max Gill Design, The Pollen Mill Florists; Paper Goods: PS Paper

PAGE 75 Photographer: Ruét Photo; Event Agency: WSE Event Agency; Florals: Layered Vintage; Stationery: Jolie & Company • Photographer: Ryan Horban Photography; Planner & Designer: Michelle Garibay Events; Design, Lighting & Florals: Arrangements Design; Stationery: Méldeen • Photographer: Krystle Akin Photography; Planner: AWE: Amazing Weddings & Events; Stationery: Ceci New York • Photographer: Lindsey Morgan Photography; Planner: Christina Kreations Wedding Planning; Florals: Lori Parker Floral Studios; Stationery: Alpine Creative Group

PAGE 76 Photographer: Ashley Cox Photography; Planner: Kim Newton Weddings; Venue: Clifton Inn; Rentals: Something Vintage Rentals • Photographer: Sarah Kate, Photographer; Planner: Pop Parties; Design & Florals: David Kimmel Design; Linen: Nuage Designs; Cakes: Fancy Cakes by Lauren

PAGE 77 Photographer: Dmitry Shumanev; Planner: Tessa Lyn Events; Florals: Butterfly Floral & Event Design; Venue: Cielo Farms; Rentals: Premiere Party Rents

PAGE 79 Photographer: John & Joseph Photography; Planner: Ashley Chanel Events; Venue: Roblar Winery

PAGE 81 Photographer: Fred Marcus Studio; Planner: Apotheosis Events; Design & Décor: David Beahm Experiences

PARTY*SLATE*

(continued)

PAGE 83 **Photographer:** Katie Lopez Photography; **Planner:** Chris Weinberg Events; **Design & Florals:** Gilded Group Décor • **Photographer:** Fred Marcus Studio; **Planner & Designer:** Norma Cohen; **Décor & Florals:** SBK Associates • **Photographer:** Heather Kincaid; **Planner:** Geller Events; **Décor:** Revelry Event Designers; **Florals:** Celio's Design • **Photographer:** Roey Yohai Studios; **Planner:** Nicky Reinhard Events; **Florals:** Stone Kelly Events

PAGE 84 **Photographer:** Daniel Colvin Photography; **Planner:** Piper & Muse Events; **Florals:** Tulipina; **Furniture:** Johanna Terry Events

PAGE 85 **Photographer:** Natalie Watson Photography; **Planner & Designer:** The Social Office; **Florals:** Artisan Bloom; **Décor:** Revelry Event Designers; **Venue:** Montage Deer Valley

PAGE 86 **Photographer:** Sarah Kate, Photographer; **Planner:** Pop Parties; **Décor & Florals:** David Kimmel Design • **Photographer:** Dmitry Shumanev; **Planner:** Natalie Sofer Weddings and Events; **Florals:** Butterfly Floral & Event Design • **Photographer:** Rachel Havel Photography; **Planner:** NYLUX Events; **Floral Design:** DesignWorks • **Photographer:** Rene Zadori; **Planner:** Fancy That Events; **Florals:** Avant Garden

PAGE 88 **Photographer:** Asher Gardner Photography; **Planner:** The Wedding Plan & Company; **Florals:** Beethoven's Veranda

PAGE 89 **Photographer:** Adam Opris Events; **Planner:** Carrie Zack Events; **Décor & Florals:** Jose Graterol Designs; **Venue:** Fontainebleau Miami Beach • **Photographer:** Donna Von Bruening; **Planner:** CONFERO • **Photographer:** Victoria Angela Photography; **Planner:** Leslie Mastin Events; **Florals:** Adam Leffel Productions • **Photographer:** Kent Drake Photography; **Planner:** Catherine Lamb Designs; **Stationery:** Elizabeth Grace

PAGE 90 **Photographer:** Sunny Lee Photography; **Planner:** The Golden Pineapple Event Company; **Production & Florals:** Petal Productions; **Venue:** The Colony Palm Beach • **Photographer:** Sunny Lee Photography; **Planner:** 59 & Bluebell Events; **Florals:** Southern Floral Company; **Venue:** The Colony Palm Beach

PAGE 91 **Photographer:** Love + Covenant Photography; **Planner:** Rackel Gehlsen Weddings & Events; **Décor & Florals:** Xquisite Events; **Venue:** The Colony Palm

Beach • **Photographer:** Blink & Co. Photography; **Planner:** Courtney Paige Events; **Décor:** Simply Events; **Venue:** The Colony Palm Beach • **Photographer:** Annie Cooper Photographer; **Planner:** The Golden Pineapple Event Company; **Florals:** Petal Productions; **Venue:** The Colony Palm Beach

PAGE 92 **Photographer:** Docuvitae; **Planner:** L'amour Events Production; **Florals:** Britlyn Simone

PAGE 93 **Photographer:** Jess Onesto; **Planner:** Stacey Goods Farm & Events • **Photographer:** MICHAEL + ANNA COSTA PHOTOGRAPHY; **Planner:** Sarah Brennan Events; **Florals:** Haute Blossoms

PAGE 94 **Photographer:** Brett Matthews Photography; **Planner:** Amy Katz Events; Design, **Décor & Florals:** Dejuan Stroud, Inc. • **Photographer:** Michael Segal Wedding Photography; **Planner:** Tessa Lyn Events; **Design & Florals:** Flower Power LA • **Photographer:** Belathée Photography; **Planner:** Arney Walker Studio; **Design & Florals:** The Style Marc • **Photographer:** Hechler Photographers; **Planner:** Forever Young Events; **Florals:** Jen Gould Event Design

PAGE 95 **Photographer:** Brett Hickman Photography; **Planner:** Nicole Alexandra Events & Designs; **Florals:** Emblem Flowers • **Photographer:** Shannon Skloss Photography; **Planner:** Julian Leaver Events; **Design:** Cassie LaMere Events; **Floral Design:** Transplants Floral

PAGE 96 **Photographer:** John & Joseph Photography; **Production & Design:** Ashley Chanel Events; **Florals:** Haute Blossom; **Venue:** Alisal Guest Ranch and Resort; **Lighting:** Bella Vista; **Rentals:** Town & Country Rentals, Theoni Collection

PAGE 97 **Photographer:** Maggie Braucher; **Planner & Designer:** Haley Kelly Events; **Florals:** Flowershop; **Rentals:** STRADLEY DAVIDSON, Snyder Event Rentals, Lola Valentina • **Photographer:** Chris J. Evans International; **Planner:** Couture Events; **Floral Design:** Teresa Sena Designs

PAGE 98 **Photographer:** Fred Marcus Studio; **Planner:** Guerdy Design; **Florals:** Birch Event Design; **Rentals:** Luxe Event Rentals; **Table Decals:** Bombshell Graphics

PAGE 99 **Photographer:** Stephania Campos Photography; **Planner:** Alyssa Meeks; **Stationery & Print:** Katie & Co.

PAGE 100 **Photographer:** Cassidy Carson; **Planner:** Fête Nashville Luxury Weddings; **Rentals:** Please Be Seated, Quest Events; **Linen:** BBJ La Tavola; **Stationery & Print:** Tenn Hens Design • **Photographer:**

Usman Baporia; **Planner:** B Beloved Events; **Design & Florals:** Flowers By Edgar; **Rentals:** Fine Linen Creation

PAGE 101 **Photographer:** Usman Baporia; **Planner:** B Beloved Events; **Design & Florals:** Flowers By Edgar; **Rentals:** Fine Linen Creation

PAGE 102 **Photographer:** Kristine Grinvalde Photography; **Planner:** Fremont Group; **Florals:** Garden of Love; **Rentals:** SOFI Design

PAGE 103 **Photographer:** Elizabeth Messina; **Planner:** Merryl Brown Events; **Rentals:** Found Rental Co. • **Photographer:** Jose Villa, Joel Serrato; **Production & Design:** Gregory Blake Sams Events, Laurie Arons Special Events; **Floral Design & Décor:** Kathleen Deery Design; **Furniture Rentals:** Found Rental Co.

PAGE 104 **Photographer:** Anya Kernes Photography; **Planner:** Callista & Company; **Florals:** Max Owens Design; **Stationery:** Lotus And Ash; **Pattern Design:** Stephanie Fishwick

PAGE 105 **Photographer:** Norman & Blake; **Planner:** Callista & Company; **Florals:** Lambert Floral Studio; **Rentals & Décor:** Theoni Collection, The Ark, Chic Event Rentals; **Stationery:** Lotus And Ash • **Photographer:** Eric Kelley Photography; **Planner:** Beth Bernstein Events; **Florals:** HMR Designs • **Photographer:** Rene Zadori; **Planner:** Mary Michelle; **Florals:** Eddie Zaratsian Lifestyle and Design • **Photographer:** Ricky Rodriguez Photography; **Planner:** Jordana Marie Events; **Floral Design:** pic and petal; **Wedding Photography Agency:** PairWed Co.

PAGE 106 **Photographer:** B Freed Photography; **Production & Design:** JOWY Productions; **Florals:** TFS Studio; **Stationery:** Annie Campbell Catering, La Artista; **Rentals:** Bright Event Rentals, Special Event Contractors, Casa De Perrin, Theoni Collection; **Props & Décor:** Revelry Event Designers, Papergarden XOXO • **Photographer:** Christy Tyler Photography; **Planner:** Nouvelle Events; **Décor:** Revel Decor; **Caterer:** Blue Plate Catering • **Photographer:** Erika Delgado; **Planner:** Your Sparkling Event; **Décor & Florals:** Renny & Reed; **Caterer:** Constellation Culinary Group

PAGE 107 **Photographer:** Katie Mangold Photography; **Planner, Décor & Florals:** Valley & Company Events; **Stationery:** Tie That Binds • **Photographer:** The Brothers Martens; **Planner:** Social Llama Events; **Caterer:** Vestals Catering • **Photographer:** Two Pair Photography;

Planner: Eclipse Event Co; **Florals:** Kitsch Floral & Event Styling; **Stationery & Print:** House of Hart Events

PAGE 109 Photographer: Nicole Piper Photography; **Planner:** Eventrics Indian Weddings; **Design & Décor:** Occasions by Shangri-la

PAGE 111 Photographer: Matthew David Studio; **Planner:** COJ Events; **Florals:** Luna Design Studios

PAGE 112 Photographer: Laura Gordon Photography; **Planner & Designer:** Nicole Alexandra Events & Designs; **Florals:** Tularosa Flowers; **Caterer:** Good Gracious! Events

PAGE 113 Photographer: Kesha Lambert; **Planner & Designer:** The Superior Collective; **Florals:** NYC Flower Project; **Caterer:** Delivering Experiences

PAGE 114 Photographer: Nico Leon; **Design:** Birch Event Design; **Caterer:** Creative Edge Parties **Photographer:** Corbin Gurkin; **Planner:** GoBella Design & Planning; **Art Direction, Décor & Florals:** Ed Libby Events; **Caterer:** Marcia Selden Catering & Events • **Photographer:** Aaron Delesie; **Planner & Designer:** David Stark Design and Production; **Caterer:** Olivier Cheng Catering • **Photographer:** Jana Williams Photography; **Planner:** Details Details; **Design & Florals:** Eucharis; **Caterer:** Good Gracious! Events • **Photographer:** Carter Rose Weddings; **Planner:** Kelly Karli Weddings & Events; **Florals:** Olive & Poppy; **Venue:** Catamount Ranch & Club

PAGE 115 Photographer: Anée Atelier; **Planner:** Cole Drake Events; **Venue:** Montage Healdsburg • **Photographer:** Michelle Walker Photography; **Planner & Designer:** Morgan Events; **Floral Design:** Flowers by Heidi; **Venue:** Four Seasons Resort Hualalai • **Photographer:** dani. fine photography; **Planner:** KG Events & Design; **Florals:** Morrice Florist; **Venue:** Harbor View Hotel • **Photographer:** Shannon Skloss Photography; **Planner:** Julian Leaver Events; **Design:** Cassie LaMere Events; **Caterer:** Savor by Samir; **Stationery:** Southern Fried Paper

PAGE 116 Photographer: Jose Villa; **Planner:** Posh Parties; **Design & Florals:** Renny & Reed; **Venue:** The Breakers Palm Beach; **Lighting:** Frost Florida

PAGE 117 Photographer: Pat Furey Photography; **Planner:** Veronica Joy Events; **Caterer:** Great Performances • **Photographer:** Britney Tarno; **Planner:** Sarabeth & Co.; **Caterer:** Vestals Catering; **Linen:** La Tavola Fine Linen • **Photographer:** Katie Lopez Photography; **Planner:** Fabuluxe Events; **Venue:** The Colony Palm Beach

PAGE 118 Photographer: Aaron Delesie; **Planner & Designer:** David Stark Design and Production; **Caterer:** Olivier Cheng Catering

PAGE 119 Photographer: Niki Marie Photography; **Planner:** Shannon Gail Events; **Venue & Caterer:** Four Seasons Hotel Chicago; **Linen:** BBJ La Tavola; **Tabletop Rentals:** Halls Rentals • **Photographer:** Shannon Skloss Photography; **Planner:** Julian Leaver Events; **Design:** Cassie LaMere Events; **Caterer:** Savor by Samir; **Tabletop:** Posh Couture Rentals; **Linen:** BBJ La Tavola; **Custom Décor:** Top Tier Staffing and Event Rentals • **Photographer:** Gregory Ross; **Planner:** Nicole Alexandra Events & Designs; **Caterer:** Good Gracious! Events

PAGE 120 Photographer: Stetten Wilson; **Planner & Designer:** Amorology; **Venue:** Park Hyatt Aviara Resort

PAGE 121 Photographer: Amy & Stuart Photography; **Planner & Designer:** Rikki Ladenheim Events; **Décor:** Revelry Event Designers; **Venue:** Hotel Bel-Air; **Linen:** Nuage Designs; **Rentals:** Town & Country Rentals, Theoni Collection • **Photographer:** Jess Onesto; **Planner:** Madix & Co.; **Caterer:** Elaine Bell Catering; **Venue:** Viansa Winery • **Photographer:** Harwell Photography; **Planner:** TOAST events; **Caterer:** Bold American Events; **Stationery:** Dear Elouise • **Photographer:** Vanessa Tierney Photography; **Planner:** Calluna Events; **Caterer:** Catering by Design; **Venue:** T-Lazy-7 Ranch

PAGE 122 Photographer: With Love & Embers; **Production:** Freed Events; **Caterer:** MAX Ultimate Food

PAGE 123 Photographer: Matt Rice Photography; **Planner:** Posh Parties; **Venue:** Faena Hotel Miami Beach • **Photographer:** Aurora Photography; **Planner & Stylist:** Pink Wasabi Events; **Caterer:** Constellation Culinary Group; **Venue:** Pérez Art Museum Miami • **Photographer:** Michelle Beller Photography; **Planner:** Alyson Fox - Alyson Fox Events; **Florals:** Mark's Garden; **Cake:** The Butter End • **Photographer:** Rebecca Theresa Photography; **Planner & Designer:** Detailed Touch Events; **Cake:** Sweet And Saucy Shop

PAGE 124 Photographer: Clane Gessel Photography; **Planner & Designer:** TYGER Productions; **Cake:** Ron Ben-Israel Cakes • **Photographer:** KingenSmith; **Planner:** Paulette Wolf Events; **Design & Florals:** HMR Designs; **Venue:** The Standard Club

PAGE 125 Photographer: Nadia D Photography; **Planner:** KIS(cubed) Events

PAGE 127 Photographer: Anna Zajac Weddings; **Planner:** The Ideal Day; **Caterer:** Big Delicious Planet

PAGE 129 Photographer: Dmitry Shumanev; **Planner:** L'amour Events Production; **Florals:** Butterfly Floral & Event Design; **Lighting & DJ:** DJ Sepi; **Venue:** Hummingbird Nest Ranch

PAGE 130 Photographer: Nathalie Cheng Photography; **Planner:** CMG Weddings and Events; **Florals:** Flower Girl Em

PAGE 132 Photographer: Nick + Lauren Photography; **Planner:** Unveiled Wedding Planning

PAGE 133 Photographer: David Turner Photography; **Planner:** Michelle Durpetti Events; **Florals:** Platinum Events

PAGE 134 Photographer: Amanda K Photo Art; **Planner:** Valley & Company Events; **Dance Floor:** LightSmiths; **Stationery & Dance Floor Design:** Lotus And Ash; **Rentals:** CORT Party Rental

PAGE 135 Photographer: Katherine Ann Rose Photography; **Planner:** The Lynden Lane Company; **Floral Design:** Pina Cate; **Rentals:** Event Design by Marianna Idrin, Ware House Rentals; **Venue:** Flora Farms • **Photographer:** Kris Kan Photography; **Planner:** Event Du Jour; **Rentals:** Revelry Event Designers; **Floral Design:** Avant Garden; **Dance Floor:** Dance Floor Depot; **Venue:** Q Vineyard; **Candles:** Vogue Candles • **Photographer:** Collin Pierson Photography; **Planner:** Clementine Custom Events; **Design & Florals:** KEHOE DESIGNS; **Venue:** Four Seasons Hotel Chicago; **Lighting & Production:** BlackOak Technical Productions • **Photographer:** Amy & Stuart Photography; **Planner & Designer:** Rikki Ladenheim Events; **Décor:** Revelry Event Designers; **Venue:** Hotel Bel-Air; **Rentals:** Town & Country Rentals, Theoni Collection; **Lighting:** Amber Event Production • **Photographer:** Lucas Rossi Photography; **Planner:** Bella Vita Events; **Florals:** Hidden Garden Flowers; **Dance Floor:** Barker Decor Service; **Candles:** Vogue Candles; **Rentals:** A Rental Connection, Hollywood Event Rentals, MTB Event Rentals, Lux Lounge EFR, 204 Events

PAGE 137 Photographer: Harwell Photography; **Planner:** TOAST events; **Florals:** Floressence Flowers; **Entertainment:** Atlanta Showstoppers; **Venue:** Cashiers Village Green; **Tent:** Professional Party Rentals; **Rentals:** Crush by Event Works

PAGE 138 Photographer: Natalie Watson Photography; **Planner & Designer:** H Three Events; **Design & Florals:** Emily Clarke Events; **Lighting:** JACOB CO

PARTY*SLATE*

(continued)

CREATIVE; **Chandeliers:** Bright Event Productions; **Linen:** Nuage Designs; **Rentals:** Please Be Seated; **Venue:** The Saint Elle • **Photographer:** Jose Villa; **Planner & Designer:** Brooke Keegan Special Events; **Florals:** Mandy Grace Design; **Venue:** Four Seasons Resort Lanai; **Entertainment:** Kapuas Entertainment, Dart Collective; **Tabletop:** Set Maui; **Lighting:** Hang Ten Lighting • **Photographer:** Shannon Skloss Photography; **Planner:** Julian Leaver Events; **Design:** Cassie LaMere Events; **Florals:** Transplants Floral; **Tabletop:** Posh Couture Rentals, Top Tier Staffing and Event Rentals; **Linen:** BBJ La Tavola; **Lighting:** LeForce Entertainment; **Venue:** The Mason Dallas • **Photographer:** Chris J. Evans International; **Venue:** Andaz Maui at Wailea

PAGE 140 Photographer: Afrik Armando; **Planner:** Lavish Haus Design + Event Co.

PAGE 141 Photographer: Jess Onesto; **Planner:** Stacey Goods Farm & Events; **Rentals:** Encore Events Rentals; **Venue:** Mountain House Estate

PAGE 143 Photographer: Shannon Griffin Photography; **Planner:** GLDN Events; **Florals:** Renny & Reed; **Entertainment:** Shea Hess; **Venue:** The Colony Palm Beach; **Tent:** Regency Party Rental & Productions

PAGE 145 Photographer: Corbin Gurkin; **Planner:** Bruce Russell Events; **Entertainment:** On The Move; **Floral Design:** Amie Bone Flowers; **Floral Production:** McCalls Catering & Events; **Structure & Design:** Hensley Event Resources

PAGE 146 Photographer: Andreas Sellinidis; **Planner:** Gold Leaf Event Design & Production; **Design:** Cerka Creative; **Entertainment:** Aragon Artists; **Lighting:** Fusion Productions

PAGE 147 Photographer: Norman & Blake; **Planner:** Callista & Company; **Entertainment:** Dart Collective; **Venue:** Ventana Big Sur • **Photographer:** Stephania Campos Photography; **Planner:** Peachy Events; **Florals:** Rose and Rae Design; **Signage:** House of Hart Events; **Audio Guest Book:** Fete Fone

PAGE 148 Photographer: Niki Marie Photography; **Planner:** Shannon Gail Events; **Décor & Florals:** Revel Decor; **Entertainment:** The Gold Coast All Stars; **Venue:** Four Seasons Hotel Chicago

PAGE 149 Photographer: Fred Marcus Studio; **Planner:** Preston Bailey; **Entertainment:** On The Move • **Photographer:** Chard Photo; **Planner &** **Designer:** Emily Clarke Events; **Entertainment:** Jordan Kahn Music Company • **Photographer:** Jacqui Cole Photography; **Planner:** Stella Day Events; **Venue:** The Colony Palm Beach • **Photographer:** Shannon Skloss Photography; **Planner:** Julian Leaver Events; **Design:** Cassie LaMere Events; **Entertainment:** Jordan Kahn Music Company

PAGE 150 Photographer: Ed & Aileen Photography; **Planner:** A Fresh Event; **Entertainment:** Knockaz Brass Band • **Photographer:** Rachel Red Photography; **Planner, Design & Florals:** Christine Janda Design & Events; **Entertainment:** Cagen Music LLC

PAGE 151 Photographer: Ushna Khan Photography; **Planner:** A Panache Affair; **Design:** Three Petals Design; **Photo Booth:** Pixster Photo Booths

PAGE 152 Photographer: Duke Images; **Design:** Stacy Porras Wedding Consulting; **Florals:** Butterfly Floral & Event Design • **Photographer:** Carter Rose Photography; **Planner:** Fabulous Fete; **Florals:** Bella Flora of Dallas; **Entertainment:** Emerald City Band

PAGE 153 Photographer: Suzanne Delawar Studios; **Planner:** Chris Weinberg Events; **Production & Décor:** Gilded Group Décor; **Venue:** The Bath Club

PAGE 155 Photographer: Tim Tab Studios; **Planner:** Bliss Events Chicago; **Floral Design:** Life In Bloom; **Entertainment:** Arlen Music Productions; **Lighting:** Elegant Event Lighting

PAGE 157 Photographer: Erika Delgado; **Planner:** Masi Events; **Décor:** Renny & Reed; **Venue:** The Colony Palm Beach

PAGE 158 Photographer: Take It Photo; **Planner:** Michigan Avenue Events; **Venue:** NIZUC Resort & Spa

PAGE 159 Photographer: Scott Clark Photo; **Planner & Designer:** Neon River Weddings; **Florals:** Designs by Ahn; **Rentals:** Patina Rentals • **Photographer:** Willett Photo; **Planner:** Drake Social; **Florals:** Amanda Jewel Floral + Design; **Venue:** The Ritz-Carlton Reynolds, Lake Oconee; **Stationery:** Hinote Studio • **Photographer:** The Brothers Martens; **Planner:** Social Llama Events; **Venue:** Bar Marilou • **Photographer:** Natalie Watson Photography; **Planner & Designer:** The Social Office; **Décor:** Revelry Event Designers; **Venue:** Montage Deer Valley

PAGE 160 & 161 Photographer: Jose Villa; **Planner & Designer:** Bustle Events; **Florals:** Tulipina; **Venue:** Blackberry Farm; **Tabletop Rentals:** The Ark Rentals; **Linen:** BBJ La Tavola; **Rentals:** Found Rental Co.; **Table Runners:** Silk & Willow; **Stationery:** Yonder Design

PAGE 162 Photographer: John & Joseph Photography; **Planner & Designer:** Ashley Chanel Events; **Venue:** Alisal Guest Ranch and Resort • **Photographer:** Katie Lopez Photography; **Planner:** Posh Parties; **Venue:** The Colony Palm Beach

PAGE 163 Photographer: One Love Photography; **Planner & Designer:** Off the Beaten Path; **Florals:** Bloom Agape; **Décor & Rentals:** Encore Events Rentals

PAGE 165 Photographer: Jose Villa, Joel Serrato; **Design & Production:** Gregory Blake Sams Events, Laurie Arons Special Events; **Floral Design & Décor:** Kathleen Deery Design; **Venue:** Montage Healdsburg; **Lighting:** Bella Vista Designs Inc; **Furniture Rentals:** Found Rental Co.; **Tabletop:** Theoni Collection; **Custom Fabrication:** Hensley Event Resources

PAGE 167 Photographer, Planner, Décor & Florals: Colin Cowie Lifestyle

PAGE 168 Photographer: Usman Baporia; **Planner & Designer:** Anaïs Event Planning & Design; **Venue:** Casa Bella

PAGE 169 Photographer: Mo Davis Photography; **Planner:** Michelle Norwood Events; **Venue:** Dos Pueblos Orchid Farm

PAGE 175 Photographer: Genevieve de Manio Photography; **Planner:** Leslie Mastin Events

want more?

Scan the code to find even more vendor credits and further inspiration at PartySlate.com

Copyright © 2024 by PartySlate, Inc.
All rights reserved.

PARTY*SLATE*

Julie Novack, CEO and Co-Founder
Lauren Mandel, VP of Marketing
Pamela Rothbard, Editorial Director
Amanda VanDagens, Associate Director of Consumer Marketing

Library of Congress Cataloging-in-Publication Data Available on request

10 9 8 7 6 5 4 3 2 1

Published by Hearst Home, an imprint of
Hearst Books/Hearst Magazine Media, Inc.
300 W 57th Street
New York, NY 10019

Jacqueline Deval, VP, Publisher
Zach Mattheus, Group Creative Director
Nicole Fisher, Deputy Director
Leah Tracosas Jenness, Project Editor
Erynn Hassinger, Cover and Interior Designer
Maria Ramroop, Deputy Managing Editor
Marc Bailes and **Vanessa Weiman,** Copyeditors

PartySlate and the PartySlate logo are the sole proprietary of PartySlate, Inc.

Hearst Home, the Hearst Home logo, and Hearst Books are registered trademarks of Hearst Communications, Inc.

For information about custom editions, special sales, premium and corporate purchases: hearst.com/magazines/hearst-books

Printed in China
978-1-958395-83-7